S A C R E D
Pathways

Also by Gary Thomas

Authentic Faith
Sacred Marriage

GARY THOMAS

SACRED
Pathways

DISCOVER YOUR
SOUL'S PATH TO GOD

ZONDERVAN

GRAND RAPIDS, MICHIGAN 49530

ZONDERVAN

Sacred Pathways
Copyright © 1996 by Gary L. Thomas
First Zondervan edition 2000

Requests for information should be addressed to:

ZondervanPublishingHouse
Grand Rapids, Michigan 49530

Library of Congress Cataloging-in-Publication Data

Thomas, Gary (Gary Lee)
    Sacred pathways : discover your soul's path to God / Gary Thomas.
        p.   cm.
    Originally published: Nashville, Tenn. : T. Nelson, c1996.
    Includes bibliographical references.
    ISBN: 0-310-24284-3 (softcover)
    1. Spiritual Life—Christianity. 2. Spirituality. 3. Temperament—Religious
aspects—Christianity. I. Title.
BV4501.2.T448 2000
248.4—dc21   99-053309
                                                                             CIP

Interior design by Korina Kelley

Printed in the United States of America

02 03 04 /❖ DC/ 10 9 8 7 6 5 4 3

For Allison and Kelsey and Graham
May you open the windows of your hearts to God's love.

ACKNOWLEDGMENTS

I'd like to thank several people for reviewing this manuscript, especially Frederica Mathewes-Green, Dr. Brian Newman, Lisa Thomas, the Reverend Brian Thorstad, and Janet Thoma. Their comments have made a significant contribution to this book. I was well served by the Zondervan staff, especially John Sloan, Heather Gemmen, and John Topliff.

I'd also like to thank my agent, Scott Waxman, and the many people who have sat through seminars and offered their suggestions to add to this material.

CONTENTS

CONTENTS

PART ONE

The Journey of the Soul

ONE

LOVING GOD

Valuable lessons about spirituality can come at the strangest times. An ear-popping flight from Washington, D.C., to Seattle, Washington, taught me a lesson I'll not soon forget. Just before I was about to embark on the trip, I came down with a severe head cold. My sinuses act up when I fly even if I'm feeling well, so I knew I needed to get some help. Since I had just moved to Virginia, I hadn't bothered to find a doctor so a coworker recommended an outpatient care clinic.

The clinic turned out to be the medical equivalent of a 7–11. I didn't have time to go anywhere else, however, so I did my best to explain my dilemma to a doctor, waited for his prescription, and left.

When I got home my wife asked me, "What did the doctor say?"

"I don't know," I responded. "I couldn't understand him."

Her eyebrows shot up. "Well, what did he prescribe?"

"I don't know. I can't read the writing."

"What kind of clinic was this?"

"I don't want to know," I said. "I have to leave town tomorrow."

The flight the next day was one of the most miserable flights of my life. It takes between four and five hours to go from Washington, D.C., to Seattle, but I was certain that my then thirty-year-old body had turned forty-five by the time I landed. My head felt like it weighed about fifty pounds.

I dutifully took the medication as it was prescribed and expected my ears to clear some by the next day, but they didn't. I wouldn't even be able to speak clearly if I didn't get some help, so after a day or two I stopped in a Portland, Oregon, clinic, hoping to obtain more relief. The new doctor put me at ease. I could understand what he was talking about and he seemed to know what he was doing. When he learned what had been prescribed for me in Virginia, his jaw dropped. "I don't know what that doctor was thinking, but I can't imagine any doctor who graduated from a United States medical school in the past thirty years prescribing this medicine for your ailment. Apparently this doctor knows just one or two medicines and is prescribing the same one for virtually everything."

This experience taught me the folly of using one medicine to treat every malady. It took some time, however, for the spiritual analogy to become clear. Over and over again we give Christians the same spiritual prescription: "You want to grow as a Christian? All you have to do is develop a thirty- or sixty-minute quiet time and come to church every Sunday morning."

All too often, Christians who desire to be fed spiritually are given the same, generic, hopefully all-inclusive methods—usually some variation on a standardized quiet time. Why? Because it's simple, it's generic, and it's easy to hold people accountable to. But, for many Christians, it's just not enough.

A.W. Tozer warns, "The whole transaction of religious conversion has been made mechanical and spiritless. We have almost forgotten that God is a person and, as such, can be cultivated as any person can."[1] The casualties of "mechanized religion" are many. It's one thing to witness spiritually empty people outside of church; what concerns me is meeting more and more Christians *inside* church who suffer this same spiritual emptiness.

Ultimately, it's a matter of spiritual nutrition. Many Christians have never been taught how to "feed" themselves spiritually. They live on a starvation diet and then are surprised that they always seem so "hungry."

Others have lapsed into routine-devotions. One of the most refreshing things that happened to my marriage was breaking my wrist. It was a serious break, requiring surgery, and thrust Lisa and me out of our routine. We did most everything together, in part because I needed so much help. Since my exercise was limited to walking, we took near-daily walks. We shopped together. We answered email together (initially, I couldn't type). For a while, Lisa even helped me get dressed. (Okay, *you* try tying your shoe with one hand!) Being out of our routine, Lisa and I discovered a deeper and newer love. The romance was always there; it had just been buried under the accretions of always doing the same thing.

The casualties of "mechanized religion" are many.

I've found that many people face the same dilemma in their walk with God. Their love for God has not dimmed, they've just fallen into a soul-numbing rut. Their devotions seem like nothing more than shadows of what they've been doing for years. They've been involved in the same ministry for so long they could practically do it in their sleep. It seems as if nobody in their small groups has had an original thought for three years. They finally wake up one morning and ask, "Is this really all there is to knowing God?"

Quiet Time Collides with Reality

Several years after I graduated from college, I realized my spiritual life had to adapt to a new schedule. I was leaving the house between 5:00 and 5:30 A.M. and getting back home around 5:30 P.M. That left an hour to have dinner with my family, an hour to spend some time with my children, half an hour to get the kids in bed, and about another hour to pay the bills, take out the garbage, catch up on my wife's day, and take phone calls. If we had an evening meeting, everything was crunched even tighter.

To have a sixty-minute quiet time, which had been a cherished staple of my spiritual diet, I would have had to get up at 4:00 A.M.! I was able to fit in some daily Bible reading before I left the house and a time of prayer during my morning commute, but I felt I was cheating. Vacations and weekends offered the opportunity to resume this discipline, but the workweek demanded something else.

This struggle to find a new "spiritual prescription" became a great blessing because I began to find new ways to nurture my soul. Perhaps the primary lesson I learned was that certain parts of me are never touched by a standardized quiet time. My discipline of quiet times was (and is) helpful; however, I came to realize that it was not sufficient. Other parts of my spiritual being lay dormant.

I also began to realize other people shared my frustration. For some people, the formulaic quiet time seems too cerebral. Others simply grow bored sitting at a desk alone in a room just reading and thinking. And why should everybody be expected to love God the same way, anyway? We would think it absurd to insist that newly evangelized Christians in Moravia create an identical worship service to Presbyterians in Boston or Baptists in Georgia. Yet we prescribe the same type of spirituality for both the farmer in Iowa and the lawyer in Washington, D.C.

Beware of Narrowing Your Approach to God

Expecting all Christians to have a certain type of quiet time can wreak havoc in a church or small group. Excited about meaningful (to us) approaches to the Christian life, we sometimes assume that if others do not experience the same thing, something must be wrong with their faith. Please, don't be intimidated by others' expectations. God wants to know the real you, not a caricature of what somebody else wants you to be. He created you with a certain personality and a certain spiritual temperament. God wants your worship, according to the way he made you. That may differ somewhat from the worship of the person who brought you to Christ or the person who leads your Bible study or church.

I must admit, there is a limit to the individual approach to spirituality. It is neither wise nor scriptural to pursue God apart from the community of faith. Our individual expressions of faith must be joined to corporate worship with the body of Christ. Fortunately, over its two thousand years of history, the church has provided us with rich and varied traditions of loving God.

Jesus accepted the worship of Peter's mother-in-law as she served him, but refused to force Mary, the sister of Martha, to also worship in that way. Mary was allowed to express her worship in the silence of adoration, not the hustle and bustle of active service. Good spiritual directors understand that people have different spiritual temperaments, that what feeds one doesn't feed all.

> *Good spiritual directors understand that people have different spiritual temperaments, that what feeds one doesn't feed all.*

Giving the same spiritual prescription to every struggling Christian is no less irresponsible than a doctor prescribing penicillin to every patient.

As I read the classics of the Christian faith and shared my journey with others, I discovered various ways people find intimacy with God: by studying church history or theology, by singing or reading hymns, by dancing, by walking in the woods. Each practice awakened different people to a new sense of spiritual vitality, and something was touched in them that had never been touched before.

This discovery put me on the track of searching out various "spiritual temperaments" as a way to explain how we each love God differently. Our spiritual temperament should be distinguished from our personality temperament, about which so much has been written. Knowing our personal temperaments, whether we are sanguine or melancholy, for instance, will tell us how we relate to others or how we can choose a suitable spouse or vocation. But it doesn't necessarily tell us how we relate to God. The focus on spiritual temperaments is an attempt to help us understand how we best relate to God so we can develop new ways of drawing near to him. My search was most influenced by biblical figures, who lived out these temperaments on the pages of Scripture, and second by historical movements within the Christian church.

One God, Many Relationships

Scripture tells us that the same God is present from Genesis through Revelation—though people worshiped that one God in many ways: Abraham had a religious bent, building altars everywhere he went. Moses and Elijah revealed an activist's streak in their various confrontations with forces of evil and in their conversations with God. David celebrated God with an enthusiastic style of worship, while his son, Solomon, expressed his love for God by offering generous sacrifices. Ezekiel and John described loud and colorful images of God, stunning in sensuous brilliance. Mordecai demonstrated his love for God by caring for others, beginning with the orphaned Esther. Mary of Bethany is the classic contemplative, sitting at Jesus' feet.

These and other biblical figures of the Old and New Testaments confirmed to me that within the Christian faith there are many different and acceptable ways of demonstrating our love for God. Our temperaments will cause us to be more comfortable in some of these expressions than others—and that is perfectly acceptable to God. In fact, by worshiping God according to the way he made us, we are affirming his work as Creator.

Historic Movements Within the Church

The second area I researched as I sought to label these spiritual temperaments was the church's historical separation into groups that agree on many larger issues, but often vehemently disagree on smaller ones. I looked into several controversies in Christian history and found that a different way of relating to God—a way hinted at through a spiritual temperament—was behind many of them. It would be simplistic to suggest that such differences were the sole or even primary cause of many church splits and denominations, but they did have some effect.

Let's take just the last five hundred years of church history. In the Middle Ages, the western branch of the church, Roman Catholicism, was steeped in the mystery of sacramental rites; Roman Catholic worship focused on the altar. When Luther theologically broke with Rome, worship was altered considerably. Luther stressed "sola Scriptura" (the sufficiency of Scripture), so he elevated the pulpit to show the importance of preaching the Word. Thus in a Reformation church, your eye would be drawn to a majestic-looking pulpit, not to an ornate altar. This change created two different styles of worship: one emphasizing the sensuous aspects of faith and the mystery of the gospel, the other emphasizing intellectual discourse in knowing, understanding, and explaining the existence of God.

The reformers differed among themselves, however. Lutherans tended to keep many of Rome's elements of worship unless those elements were overtly rejected by Scripture. Calvinists tended to get rid of every element unless it was prescribed in Scripture.

The different ways of loving God extended even to how that love was expressed in the world. Calvinists rejected the monastic expression of loving God—a strict separation from society—and opted instead to express love for God by transforming society. The line between church and state began to blur. Calvin wanted Christians to hold the important offices of the state, and even went so far as to execute a heretic.

The Anabaptists, on the other hand, sought to express their love for God by stressing the inner reality of the gospel. They became separatists and pacifists, refusing to participate in the affairs of secular government. Instead, they attempted to create a model society that would witness to the unbelieving world by inviting them to come out of the secular society and join the community of faith.

All four players—Roman Catholics, Lutherans, Calvinists, and Anabaptists—were trying to love God, but with unique expressions of that love. Many differences had theological roots, but some were also related to worship preferences.

John Wesley, an eminent Anglican, was humbled on a transocean trip as he witnessed the faith of the Moravians, who bravely maintained their serenity in the face of death. In response, Wesley traded in a faith based on creeds and discipline for the inner faith displayed by the Moravians, and began preaching the necessity of relating to God through an inward transformation. Thus Methodism was born.

In the early part of the twentieth century, the Azusa street revival brought Pentecostal practices back into common church life. Today, virtually every congregation has been influenced by the charismatic renewal, whether they agree with Pentecostal theology or not. The singing of choruses and the clapping or raising of hands have spread to virtually every denomination.

At the same time inner experience was meeting with Pentecostal elements, another wing of the church began stressing the social obligations of the gospel—and the Social Gospel movement was born, with one wing promoting prohibition and the other wing, socialism. In this expression of Christianity, what counted was loving your neighbor and creating a just society, not having vague, inner experiences of spiritual delight.

Instead of learning from others, Christians have often chosen to segregate themselves by starting a new church whenever worship preferences diverge. This segregation has erected denominational walls and impoverished many Christians. Unless you happen to be born into just the right tradition, you're brought up to feed on somebody else's diet. Unfortunately, some Christians have a tendency to question the legitimacy of any experience that may not particularly interest them. Instead of saying, "That's not for me," they proclaim, "That shouldn't be for anybody."

> *Instead of learning from others, Christians have often chosen to segregate themselves by starting a new church whenever worship preferences diverge.*

This is not unlike an attitude expressed one time by my home schooled daughter who was struggling with a math problem that her mother had assigned her: Allison lamented, "This is too hard. It's not fair! In fact, I'm quite sure it's unbiblical!"

Of course, there is nothing "unbiblical" about math, but this same attack is often adopted when we question experiences that other Christians have—particularly experiences that strike us as "weird." I'm talking about "theologically neutral" practices here. For instance, one woman may discover that incense helps her to pray, while another woman thinks using incense is just plain weird. The two can agree to disagree without making a theological issue out of a doctrinally neutral worship preference.

God has given us different personalities and temperaments. It's only natural that these differences should be reflected in our worship.

Personality Temperaments

Carl Jung developed four profiles to describe human nature. (These profiles have been formulated by Isabel Briggs Myers in the popular Myers Briggs test.) First, we approach reality either as an *extrovert*, who is most at home in the social world, or as an *introvert*, who prefers to dwell in the inner world. Second, we register input as either a *sensing* person, using the five senses, or an *intuitive* person, using the imagination. Third, we organize and arrange data either as a *thinking* person, who uses logic and the intellect, or as a *feeling* person who

> A sacred pathway . . . describes the way we relate to God, how we draw near to him.

arranges data according to how it affects people and relates to human values. Finally, we arrange our outer reality as either a *judging* person, who is orderly, controlling, and managing, or a *perceptive* person, who is spontaneous and flexible. Combinations of these four profiles can create sixteen different personality types, and the Myers Briggs test is designed to separate these types.[2]

While spiritual temperaments differ from personality temperaments, Briggs' "types" can point us to different ways that we relate to the God who created us with a variety of dispositions and inclinations. Using biblical figures, historic church movements, and various personality temperaments, we can identify nine spiritual temperaments—what I call sacred pathways.

Sacred Pathways: An Overview

What is a "sacred pathway"? Put very simply, it describes the way we relate to God, how we draw near to him. Do we have just one pathway? Not necessarily. Most of us, however, will naturally have a certain predisposition for relating to God, which is our predominant spiritual temperament.

The Nine Sacred Pathways

Here is a short overview of the nine spiritual temperaments. Part two of this book will launch into a detailed look at each temperament. As you read through these nine sacred pathways you might check the ones that apply to you.

Naturalists: Loving God Out of Doors

Naturalists would prefer to leave any building, however beautiful or austere, to pray to God beside a river. Leave the books behind, forget the demonstrations—just let them take a walk through the woods, mountains, or open meadows.

These Christians believe that nature clearly proclaims "God is!" They may learn more from watching an ant colony or looking at a peaceful lake than from reading a book or listening to a sermon, though they may find fulfilling thoughts from the parables of Christ, which are based on nature, or the Psalms.

Naturalists are related to contemplatives, except that they are moved by creation in addition to the inner world. When they are out of doors, their heart soars to worship God. A modern-day example might be the writer Annie Dillard. In her book *Holy the Firm,* Dillard wrote, "I know only enough of God to want to worship him, by any means ready to hand."[3] One of her primary means was spending time out of doors. Perhaps because Dillard fell in love with the Pacific Northwest, where I grew up, I have a particular affinity for her works. I've also lived in Virginia, where Dillard camped out in the Blue Ridge Mountains and recorded that now famous and moving scene of a moth flying into a candle's flame.

From these ordinary events and scenes—moths, mountains, and the Puget Sound—Dillard uncovered the mystery of the holy, transcendent God. She wrote that she visited the Cascade range "to study hard things, rock mountain and salt sea, and to temper my spirit on their edges."

"Teach me thy ways, O Lord" is, like all prayers, a rash one, and one I cannot but recommend. These mountains, Mount Baker and the Sisters and Shuksan, the Canadian Coastal Range and the Olympics on the Peninsula, are surely the edge of the known and comprehended world. They are high. That they bear their own unimaginable masses and weathers aloft, holding them up in the sky for anyone to see plain, makes them, as Chesterton said of the Eucharist, only the more mysterious by their very visibility and absence of secrecy. They are the eastern rim of the real, if not considerably beyond it.[4]

Like Dillard, naturalists learn to seek God by surrounding themselves with all that he has made. Notice how the physical beauty that surrounds Dillard continually mirrors the spiritual, unseen faith within her.

Sensates: Loving God with the Senses

Sensate Christians want to be lost in the awe, beauty, and splendor of God. They are drawn particularly to the liturgical, the majestic, the grand. When these Christians worship, they want to be filled with sights, sounds, and smells that overwhelm them. Incense, intricate architecture, classical music, and formal language send their hearts soaring.

> Sensate Christians . . . are drawn particularly to the liturgical, the majestic, the grand. . . . Incense, intricate architecture, classical music, and formal language send their hearts soaring.

Whereas some Christians might find such a sensuous onslaught distracting, these Christians delight in it. The five senses are God's most effective inroad to their hearts.

W. Phillip Keller, author of the popular book *A Shepherd Looks at Psalm 23*, strikes me as someone with sensate tendencies. In his book *Taming Tension*, Keller writes about being a university student confined to a "rather cramped and drab home" one winter. He found escape in a picture of a "magnificent sunset scene. Again and again I absorbed myself in its loveliness. It was a tremendous uplift and inspiration amid what otherwise would have been unbearable surroundings."[5]

In the same book Keller talks about the role of music in his life. During his self-described "lonely years" in a foreign land, Keller took out his violin "to ease the heartache and inner pain. An hour of music making would set my heart to singing again." He found that "even such a simple habit as humming or whistling can turn a doleful day into one filled with new hope and good cheer."

Once Keller fully understood the meaning of Handel's *Messiah*, he began playing it year-round. "At times when I am downcast or despondent over life's sufferings, the melodies and message of this music, showing how Christ Himself also felt such grief and sorrow, have lifted me in a way that no other human agency could possibly have done."

Sight and music, among other things, have played key roles in bringing Keller into new realms of worship and fellowship with God. Anything that touches the senses can be a powerful arbiter of worship for sensate Christians.

Traditionalists: Loving God Through Ritual and Symbol

Traditionalists are fed by what are often termed the historic dimensions of faith: rituals, symbols, sacraments, and sacrifice. These Christians tend to have a disciplined life of faith. Some may be seen by others as legalists, defining their faith largely by matters of conduct. Frequently they enjoy regular attendance at church services, tithing, keeping the Sabbath, and so on.

Traditionalists have a need for ritual and structure. The contemplatives' unstructured "prayer of the quiet" would be confusing and fairly unfulfilling to them.

Rod Dreher, a movie reviewer for the *New York Post,* is a traditionalist. Dreher grew up attending informal Christian worship services. The emotional fervor of these services attracted him to the faith, but they weren't able to hold him—and his commitment fell off during his days in boarding school. A brush with some modern-day Christian writings eventually led Dreher back to the faith, but this time he found himself craving more established ritual and structure. Much to his surprise, he soon found that liturgies weren't confining and dead, as he had supposed they were, but rather carried a depth and historicity that added a new aesthetic to his worship. "It was more beautiful than anything I had ever experienced," he said.

Dreher was drawn by the ritual, and he was moved by the fact that he was praying prayers that had been prayed by many Christians in earlier centuries. The structure of the services brought more discipline to his personal life. Experiencing the same ritual week after week has deepened his understanding of the faith and his commitment to it.

Now Dreher says, "I live more liturgically in my everyday life. It's created a greater depth and texture to my Christian faith."

Ascetics: Loving God in Solitude and Simplicity

Ascetics want nothing more than to be left alone in prayer. Take away the liturgy, the trappings of religion, the noise of the outside world. Let there be nothing to distract them—no pictures, no loud music—and leave them alone to pray in silence and simplicity.

Ascetics live a fundamentally internal existence. Even when they are part of a group of people, they might seem to be isolated from the others. Frequently introspective, sometimes to a fault, they are uncomfortable in any environment that keeps them from "listening to the quiet."

Singer and writer Michael Card is a good example of the ascetic temperament. He lives in a Shaker-inspired home on one hundred acres in a rural part of Franklin, Tennessee. Card admires the Shaker emphasis on simplicity in architecture and lifestyle. His dream is to establish a small, silent retreat center on his land where pastors, artists, and songwriters could spend time with the Lord in prayer and fasting.

The lyrics of Card's songs, like the reprise in "The Things We Leave Behind," often advocate the simple life:

Every heart needs to be set free
From possessions that hold it so tight
'Cause freedom's not found in the things that we own
It's the power to do what is right
With Jesus, our only possession
Then giving becomes our delight
And we can't imagine the freedom we find
From the things we leave behind.

Activists: Loving God Through Confrontation

Activists serve a God of justice, and their favorite Scripture is often the account of Jesus cleansing the temple. They define *worship* as standing against evil and calling sinners to repentance. These Christians often view the church as a place to recharge their batteries so they can go back into the world to wage war against injustice.

Activists may adopt either social or evangelistic causes, but they find their home in the rough-and-tumble world of confrontation. They are energized more by interaction with others, even in conflict, than by being alone or in small groups.

> *Activists . . . often view the church as a place to recharge their batteries so they can go back into the world to wage war against injustice. . . . They are energized . . . by interaction with others, even in conflict.*

Francis Schaeffer is a good example of this temperament. Though he was known primarily as a "thinker," Schaeffer's thoughts usually led to activism. In his seminal work *How Shall We Then Live?* Francis Schaeffer wrote that "as Christians we are not only to *know* the right world view but consciously to *act* upon that world view so as to influence society in all its parts and facets across the whole spectrum of life, as much as we can to the extent of our individual and collective ability." Schaeffer goes on to commend great Christian activists such as Elizabeth Fry, Lord Shaftesbury, William Wilberforce, and John Wesley.[6]

Schaeffer believed that truth equals confrontation. Once an idea is unleashed, it has the power to change society, he said. His book *What-*

ever Happened to the Human Race?, cowritten with C. Everett Koop, was one of the first contemporary evangelical books to point out the wrong of abortion and to encourage Christians to active opposition. Schaeffer lived his beliefs; he played a significant role in helping to found one of the most strategic prolife organizations still operating today (Care Net).

Caregivers: Loving God by Loving Others

Caregivers serve God by serving others. They often claim to see Christ in the poor and needy, and their faith is built up by interacting with other people. Such Christians may find the devotional lives of contemplatives and enthusiasts as selfish. Whereas caring for others might wear many of us down, this recharges a caregiver's batteries.

Perhaps the supreme example of this temperament is Mother Teresa of Calcutta (born Agnes Gonxha Bojaxhiu), who at the age of twelve was so struck by the accounts of poverty in India, she decided to be a Roman Catholic missionary. In 1946, as a member of a community of Irish nuns working in the Moti Jhul slums of Calcutta, she heard God's call to change course: "I was to leave the convent and help the poor, while living among them."[7]

In 1950 she became an Indian citizen and founded her Missionaries of Charity as part of the Archdiocese of Calcutta. Many Americans do not realize that her work now extends to this country and throughout the world. Today some four thousand nuns recognized by their white saris, small crucifixes, and spartan lifestyle run approximately five hundred convents in eighty-seven countries. Nuns work in inner-city convents in New York, Washington, Atlanta, Los Angeles, and thirty other United States cities, feeding the hungry, housing the homeless, and caring for the diseased.

When she dedicated a convent in Charlotte, North Carolina, in 1995, Mother Teresa said, "God died for you and for me and for that leper and for that person dying of hunger and for that person on the street. . . . It's not enough to say you love God. You also have to say you love your neighbor. Love, to be true, has to hurt. This requires people giving until it hurts. Otherwise it is not true love. . . . Be the good news to your home people first. Find out about your next-door neighbor."[8]

Enthusiasts: Loving God with Mystery and Celebration

Excitement and mystery in worship is the spiritual lifeblood of enthusiasts. As sensates want to be surrounded by beauty and intellectuals want to be grappling with concepts, enthusiasts are inspired by joyful celebration. These Christians are cheerleaders for God and the Christian life. Let them clap their hands, shout "Amen!" and dance in their excitement, that's all they ask.

If their hearts aren't moved, if they don't experience God's power, something is missing. They don't want to just know concepts, but to experience them, to feel them, and to be moved by them.

The writer Ann Kiemel Anderson strikes me as someone who well fits this profile, though she might also fit in one or two others. Anderson's love of spending time with children, which shows her playful and childlike spirit, her delight in celebrative songs, and her belief in the power of God's mystery to work out everything according to his will are all hallmarks of a true enthusiast.

> *Enthusiasts are . . . cheerleaders for God and the Christian life. . . . They don't want to just know concepts, but to experience them, to feel them, and to be moved by them.*

Contemplatives: Loving God Through Adoration

Contemplatives refer to God as their lover, and images of a loving Father and Bridegroom predominate their view of God. Their favorite Bible passages might be taken from the Song of Songs as they enter the "divine romance." The focus is not necessarily on serving God, doing his will, accomplishing great things in his name, or even obeying God. Rather, these Christians seek to love God with the purest, deepest, and brightest love imaginable.

It's difficult to give a well-known, modern-day example of a contemplative since a true contemplative is not going to seek the spotlight. However, virtually every Christian is familiar with the biblical account of Mary of Bethany, who sat and worshiped at Jesus' feet and was commended by Jesus for doing so. If you love this story and feel a kindred spirit with Mary, you may be a contemplative.

Intellectuals: Loving God with the Mind

Intellectuals might be skeptics or committed believers, but in either case they are likely to be studying (and, in some instances, arguing either for or against) doctrines like Calvinism, infant baptism, ordination of women, and predestination. These Christians live in the world of concepts.

Some intellectuals, influenced by a personality type that may be shy or withdrawn, might avoid intellectual confrontation but still be "fed" primarily by intellectual activity. "Faith" is something to be understood as much as experienced. They may feel closest to God when they first understand something new about him.

There are many well-known and well-respected Christian intellectuals in our own time, including Dr. J. I. Packer and Dr. R. C. Sproul. Though Dr. Packer has earned the respect of academic theologians worldwide, he continues to make the doctrines of academics accessible and useful to the people in the pew. His classic books, such as *Knowing God*[9] and *Keep in Step with the Spirit*,[10] are popular studies that make difficult theological discussions understandable to even the newest Christian.

> *One of the ways to determine your dominant spiritual temperament is to list those Christians whom you most admire and seek to emulate.*

One of the ways to determine your dominant spiritual temperament is to list those Christians whom you most admire and seek to emulate. How would you describe each one? If you consistently find yourself picking leaders of a particular spiritual temperament, you may share that makeup.

Complete Christians

Imagine that General H. Norman Schwarzkopf, Queen Elizabeth, Beethoven, Chuck Swindoll, Twila Paris, and the poet Robert Browning were all rolled into one. What would you have? King David!

Think about it. He was a military general, a political ruler, a composer, a religious leader, a musician, and a poet. He was a true

Renaissance man thousands of years before European culture invented one!

David exemplified what many moderns would consider contradictory qualities. Contemporary scholars would put military and religious leaders—Genghis Khan and St. Francis of Assisi, for instance—on opposite ends of the scale; but David was able to fulfill both roles, and more.[11]

> *If you are in a spiritual malaise, it might be that you just need a change in your spiritual diet.*

"Ideal" Christians might display many, if not all, of the spiritual temperaments. As we describe each one in detail in later chapters, you'll notice that I cite Jesus as an example of all of them. Regardless of our predominant spiritual temperament, all of us could learn a great deal from how others are nourished by God and how others meet and love God.

Once you've gone through this book, you'll be able to express your own spiritual temperament or temperaments. Knowing this, you can begin a program of feeding yourself spiritually. The goal here is not self-actualization or spiritual self-absorption, but to feed our souls so we can know God in a new way, love him with every cell of our being, and then express that love by reaching out to others.

If you are in a spiritual malaise, it might be that you just need a change in your spiritual diet. If you just can't seem to leave that one particular sin, you may find that the answer is very simple: You don't know how to be nourished according to the way God made you so you're seeking spiritual "junk food," in the form of sin or addictions, somewhere else. Finding fulfillment in God is the most powerful antidote to any sin.

Some people who have read this book have found that they strongly identify with one particular type. Others have "charted" their faith: "I started out as an enthusiast, became a contemplative, and ended up a sensate." Within all of us, however, there needs to be a common denominator, which is found in Mark 12:30.

According to Jesus, four elements are essential to every true expression of faith. It is essential that we love God with all our heart (adoration), soul (will), mind (belief), and strength (body). The intellectual is not excused from failing to adore. Neither is the contemplative excused from harboring wrong beliefs about God. Complete Christians—which all of us are called to be—should exhibit adoration, belief, commitment, and service.

It might be tempting to just read the chapters that talk about your own particular spiritual temperament, but I believe you may find that your life hasn't expressed certain temperaments because you've never been exposed to them. That's certainly what I discovered in my search. By reading all the chapters, you'll gain a much more comprehensive view of how Christians have learned to express their love for God. You may even find that your initial evaluation of yourself proves to be not so accurate.

By understanding our spiritual temperaments, we can develop the tools we need to grow spiritually. These tools will differ, of course—a ten-year-old girl who loves to paint and sing and draw pictures for Jesus will have a different way of relating to God than a construction worker who is trying to figure out how being a Christian affects the way he builds houses ten to twelve hours a day.

We need to be careful, however, when we talk about "tools." Language is frequently imprecise, and no less so than when we're talking about spiritual matters. It would be easy to make a caricature out of what we're saying, reducing a dynamic relationship with the Holy God—in which he is the initiator and the sustainer—into a bunch of formulas and trick tests. But that's not what this study is all about.

The aim of this book is to help people understand the Spirit that God gave them. Good spiritual counselors don't heal anyone, they try to bring the troubled soul into God's presence, remove the confusion and subterfuge of sin and self, and let God's Spirit have his way. And that's what this book is attempting to do.

Married to God

After many people in a certain congregation read my first book, *Seeking the Face of God*, I was invited to speak at their church retreat. Prior to my arrival, I received quite a few letters in which various members stated their high expectations. At the start of the first talk,

I did my best to squash those expectations. "It would be very easy to manipulate a mountaintop experience over the course of this weekend," I told them. "Working with the worship leader, setting the right schedule, having a carefully coordinated teaching progression, we could create a spiritual high if we wanted to.

"But after praying rather substantially about this weekend, I became convinced that I am not here to offer you a mind-blowing 'date' with God. I want us to talk about how to be married to him— about how, through the ups and downs and the routine of life, we can learn to spend time with God, enjoy him, and be conformed to his will. Anybody can 'date' God. The truly mature seek to be his faithful, lifelong companions."

That's my attitude in writing this book. How do we learn to love God, day in and day out, through the seasons of life? How do we keep this love fresh? How do we grow in our adoration and understanding of God?

We do it by spending time with him. And once we understand the myriad ways that Christians have cultivated this relationship, we'll have more ideas than we need to walk closer, and more constantly, by his side.

Let's now turn our attention to these very simple but powerful spiritual temperaments.

PART TWO

The Nine Sacred Pathways

TWO

NATURALISTS: LOVING GOD OUT OF DOORS

One Christmas Eve afternoon I escaped to walk through a favorite part in the woods on the outskirts of Manassas, Virginia. The quiet, motionless world was a welcomed change from the butting and clawing of the department stores and malls. The stillness created a sense of expectancy of the birth of Christ, which was far removed from the hurry and worry of the artificial hoopla of the increasingly secularized Christmas holiday.

The woods broke into a clearing and I pulled my coat tighter as the cold wind licked at my neck. The gusts blew around me, picking up momentum, and then suddenly burst forth into snow. I turned my back to the biting wind, pulled my hood up to cover my neck, and watched the wind carry the snow along the ground, making it travel some distance before it could rest. My heart nearly stopped as I was overcome by the sheer beauty. The snow lasted only minutes. My wife, just a few miles away at our home, didn't see any snow at all. Those few, priceless moments did more to draw me into a remembrance of the Christ child than did weeks in shopping malls, post offices, and gaudily decorated rooms.

This experience helped me to begin looking at creation as God's cathedral. I continue to have the vast majority of my daily devotions indoors, but many are tied to the remembrance (and anticipation) of worshiping God outside, in his cathedral. These memories can be powerful, remaining with us long after their first light has faded away. Francis of Assisi composed his famous poem "The Canticle to Brother Sun"—perhaps *the* Christian classic on the beauty and glory of creation—when an eye infection had rendered him almost totally blind.[1]

As I read the histories of other Christians, I found that I am not alone in my desire to worship and learn of God out of doors. As a young man, the great eighteenth-century revivalist, Jonathan Edwards, wrote a monograph on the flying spiders of the North American forests. A number of years later, in one of the most famous sermons ever preached on American soil, Edwards used the analogy of a spider hanging by a thin web to depict an unrepentant sinner's dilemma in the hands of an angry God. Edwards is just one of many Christians who learned to use God's creation to understand God the Creator and his ways with men and women.

Where we worship can have a profound impact on the quality of our worship.

Where we worship can have a profound impact on the quality of our worship. The naturalist seeks to leave the formal architecture and the padded pews to enter an entirely new "cathedral," a place that God himself has built: the out-of-doors.

Any place that has some trees or a stream or, at minimum, open skies, can be God's cathedral. Naturalists have found that getting outside can literally flood parched hearts and soften the hardest soul. While it may be impractical for most congregations to regularly meet outside, individual worshipers or small groups can find great benefit in slipping away to a quiet spot to meet with God out of doors.

Naturalists in the Bible

It should be obvious, though modern conveniences hid the truth from me for so long, that the Bible is meant to be read outside. Many Old Testament and Gospel illustrations and allusions are based on nature, and it is only in the context of nature that they regain their meaning and force. The phrase "river of life" seems quaint when the words are projected up on a wall; but its power is nearly overwhelming when you stand by a swiftly flowing river. "Green pastures" can sound almost postcardish until you enter an unspoiled meadow, far away from the sound of a highway, radio, or ball game.

When God created a paradise for the first man and woman, was it a resort house? A fancy motel? An elaborate palace? No. God chose to walk with Adam and Eve in a garden.

I'll give up the artificial glare of an overhead projector for the sun's light peeking over a rise any day. I'd much rather hear the howl of a strong wind racing over the earth than the clank of the heater kicking on in the middle of a sermon. When we lock ourselves inside, we leave part of God's creation, and therefore part of our understanding, outside. Artificial comfort comes to us at a cost.

Many of the Old Testament "theophanies," or appearances of God, happened in the wilderness.[2] God met Hagar in the desert, Abraham on a mountain, Jacob at a river crossing, and Moses at a burning bush. It was far less common for God to visit someone in an urban center.

Jesus himself seems to have sought out the beauty of creation. Early in his ministry, he moved from Nazareth to live in Capernaum, which is by the sea.[3] When he called some of his disciples to follow him, he was walking by the Sea of Galilee.[4]

Jesus often taught in the countryside, and he very well may have been pointing to the images as he taught. Who is to say that birds weren't flying overhead when he talked of God's care for them? Or that he wasn't actually pointing to real flowers when he talked of their beauty? Unfortunately we have moved baptism from the river to the blue tub behind the pulpit. We hear the pastor read the

Sermon on the Mount as he stands on top of carpeted stairs instead of sitting on a hillside covered with green grass. Worship has moved from Mount Sinai with all its sights, sounds, and smells to a painted room designed to "protect" us from outside distractions.[5] And we have endured months of building-fund appeals to achieve this "progress"!

When God created a paradise for the first man and woman, was 0it a resort house? A fancy motel? An elaborate palace? No. God chose to walk with Adam and Eve in a garden with plentiful trees and a beautiful river with four river heads.

The Spiritual Lessons of the Out-of-doors

Naturalists often learn their best lessons in the out-of-doors. Three particularly come to mind: they visualize scriptural truths, they see God more clearly, and they learn to rest.

Visualizing Scriptural Truths

One day in January, I made my way through a meadow. Though much of the woods around me was barren, the tall grass had taken on a reddish tint. Examining a single blade of grass, I saw that each one by itself was an ugly grayish-brown color, but together they created a beautiful, rusty-looking hue. Immediately I thought of the connection between us as individual Christians and the nature of the church body, which reflects God's glory.

The trail took me up another small hill, and at the top I was greeted by a clear view of the Virginia countryside, with rolling hills and wide meadows. I thought back to my days in Washington State, with the perpetually snow-topped mountains, the evergreens, the much larger rivers and waterfalls, and I wondered which was more beautiful. Would I take the meadows, the rolling hills, and the tiny creeks of Virginia or the evergreen forests of Washington State with their fern-covered floors and imposing mountains that twist the highways with their impenetrable rock bases? I couldn't decide—and that's when I learned another valuable lesson by being out of doors:

God's beauty isn't limited. How different this is, I thought as I stood in God's cathedral, from "Hollywood-beauty" where all the leading women need the same color of hair and roughly the same shape of body and the men need to craft a certain physique and master the same gnarling scowl.

I caught just a flashing glimpse of the difference between an infinite God and finite men and women. The glimpse was too sudden to hold on to, but strong enough to humble me under my limitations and encourage me with God's great possibilities.

The lessons we can learn out of doors are waiting for us every day—a whole new cast coming to town with each changing season. Jonathan Edwards was fond of creation analogies and entitled an entry in his notebook "The Language and Lessons of Nature." The fact that roses have thorns, he said, teaches us that "all temporal sweets are mixt with bitter." Spiders sucking flies represent the devil and temptation; rivers running to the ocean are symbols of all things tending toward God.[6]

If you feel like your time in front of books or listening to sermons has become stagnant, grab a coat, pick up a walking stick, and step outside into a school that never closes.

Francis of Assisi was famous for his care of worms, which reminded him of the description of the humiliated Savior in Psalm 22:6: "I am a worm and not a man, scorned by men and despised by the people." Bernard of Clairvaux, a famous Cistercian monk and follower of Francis of Assisi, wrote, "You will find more laboring in the woods than you ever will among books. Woods and stones will teach you what you can never hear from any master."[7]

Anthony (born A.D. 251), an ascetic made famous by the writings of Athanasius, was once asked, "How . . . dost thou content thyself, father, who are denied the comfort of books?"

Anthony replied, "My book, philosopher, is the nature of created things, and as often as I have a mind to read the words of God, it is at my hand."[8]

God will speak to us through creation if we'll only listen. If you feel like your time in front of books or listening to sermons has become stagnant, grab a coat, pick up a walking stick, and step outside into a school that never closes.

When you do so, you will also see God more clearly.

Seeing God More Clearly

In 1998, seventy-seven-year-old John Glenn returned to space. Almost immediately, he was overwhelmed with the presence of God. "Looking at the Earth from this vantage point," he told reporters, "looking at this kind of creation and to not believe in God, to me, is impossible."

Glenn is not alone. Space flight apparently is a rather effective evangelist. Bryan O'Connor, a retired astronaut, said an enhanced faith "is pretty common" for astronauts. "I can tell you I felt a sense of awe out there looking at the Earth that I never had before."[9]

This shouldn't surprise us. "The heavens declare the glory of God; the skies proclaim the works of his hands," declares the psalmist.[10] The apostle Paul writes, "For since the creation of the world God's invisible qualities are clearly seen, being understood from what has been made."[11]

Christian confessions and individuals have attested to the scriptural truth that God is often revealed and encountered out of doors. Article two of the Reformed tradition's *Belgic Confession* says that God is made known to us "by the creation, preservation, and government of the universe; which is before our eyes as a most elegant book, wherein all creatures great and small, are as so many characters leading us to see clearly the invisible things of God."

The famous preacher Charles Haddon Spurgeon put it this way: "Surely, everything that comes from the hand of such a Master-artist as God has something in it of himself! There are lovely spots on this fair globe which ought to make even a blasphemer devout. I have said, among the mountains, 'He who sees no God here is mad.' There are things that God has made which overwhelm with a sense of his omnipotence: how can men see them, and doubt the existence of the Deity?"

John Milton, in his famous poem, "Paradise Lost," wrote, "In contemplation of created things/By steps we may ascend to God."[12]

And one of the great hymns of the faith, "How Great Thou Art," celebrates the way creation calls us to God:

> When through the woods, and forest glades I wander,
> I hear the birds sing sweetly in the trees;
> When I look down from lofty mountain grandeur
> And hear the brook and feel the gentle breeze;
> Then sings my soul, my Savior God, to thee,
> How great thou art! How great thou art!

The existence, wonder, and worthiness of God are broadcast daily for all to see if we will simply step outside and open our minds and hearts to the truth.

More than just the beauty of God is revealed outside, however. His awful and fearful terror is revealed as well. The Bible teaches us that God is a God of mercy and grace, but he is also a God of justice and judgment. It's not a surprise, then, that the same rain that nourishes the ground can disintegrate a coastline in a tropical storm. The same sun that feeds vegetation in the spring can burn fragile plants in the summer. The same wind that keeps us cool in the summer can send our houses sailing during a spring tornado.

Let creation remind us of God's beauty and let it also remind us of God's power and judgment.

Finally let nature bring us closer to God's peace by learning to rest in him.

Learning to Rest

This aspect of creation is particularly close to my heart. On one occasion I was near burnout and faced a six-week stretch of five out-of-town trips, two of them cross-country. Someone came into my office and asked me to make a decision on a relatively simple matter. I just stared at him. "I'll get back with you," I said.

Recognizing my precarious condition, I took a long lunch, walking through Two Chimneys Park in Falls Church, Virginia, then out through an established neighborhood with mature trees, and finally circling Cherry Hill Park. It was a cold day, but the chill helped me to wake up. Leaves crunched under my feet, the trees cast their steadiness into my soul, and the distant sun smiled some perspective into my troubled mind.

I poured out my heart to God. "I just can't do this," I said. "It's too much, balancing work, my family, my writing, my speaking schedule, and everything else. I'm ready to quit." Yet after praying and being outside, I was able to face the office for the rest of the day. And within days, God answered my prayers by providentially canceling two of the engagements, mercifully overcoming my lack of discretion in committing myself to such a schedule in the first place.

> *Jesus knew that God is our caregiver, but creation can be the warm blanket that God uses to wrap our cold hearts.*

As I walked around that park I also realized: We don't always need a change. Sometimes, we just need a rest, and there is no better place to rest our bodies and our souls than outside.

In Psalm 23, David credits God with restoring his soul, but clearly, the pastoral setting plays a role.[13] The out-of-doors cannot replace fellowship with God, but it can be used by God in powerful ways. Susan Power Bratton, a Christian writer and naturalist, writes:

> Experiencing the beauty and peace of God in nature is not a substitute for direct interaction with the regenerative powers of the Creator, but . . . the mending and binding so necessary to heal our stress filled lives may flow through creation. For the spiritually oppressed or the socially injured, a pleasing or quiet natural environment can help provide spiritual release. Resting by a clear, free-running river or sitting on a sunny slope in blooming desert grassland can bring peace and joy into very clouded souls.[14]

In the midst of a busy schedule of ministry, Jesus often sought lonely places to pray and be replenished. He taught his disciples to do the same.[15] It may be just a coincidence in this instance, but it's interesting that Jesus and his disciples departed by boat to rest; being "coddled" by the water is a most refreshing experience. Jesus knew that God is our caregiver, but creation can be the warm blanket that God uses to wrap our cold hearts.

How to Love God Out of Doors

The sun cast crystal rays off the water on a late summer day in Birch Bay, just below the Canadian border and about one hundred miles north of Seattle, Washington. The water that day was calm and gently lapped at the sides of my kayak. A small baby couldn't have been more comfortable at her mother's breast.

Steve, a college friend who was now a pastor, pulled his kayak close to mine. We stopped paddling and let ourselves be rocked by the small, graceful waves. Then we talked of how life had changed for us over the past dozen years. We talked of what God was doing in our lives, how we felt challenged and how we felt encouraged. We talked about mutual friends, we laughed, we thanked God, we appreciated each other's company and the world that God had given us in which to enjoy it.

As we paddled back toward the shore, I marveled at what I had missed growing up. My boyhood home was farther south of the Bay, under the shadow of Mount Rainier. The Pacific Northwest's evergreen forests are one of the strongest memories of my childhood.

I was in the forests a lot, but most of the time I was running. My heart hadn't grown to the point where I could enter a forest and think of it as God's cathedral, a sacred place of prayer. In our modern age, where we're born in the antiseptic environment of a hospital, taken home to a nursery that consists of Sheetrock coated with paint, and driven through the countryside in a metal contraption called a car, our ability to appreciate and meet God in creation is stunted, to say the least.

One writer observed, "Nothing prevents us from experiencing this universally miraculous character of the creation, except our failure to order our affections rightly and to use our senses."[16] In other words, we need to be spiritually reawakened to fully appreciate the out-of-doors. Elizabeth Barrett Browning understood this when she wrote the now famous words:

Earth's crammed with heaven and every common bush afire
with God.
But only he who sees takes off his shoes/The rest sit round it
and pick blackberries.

How can we be reawakened to this? I have some ideas since I've traveled from being a Cub Scout who used to romp through the woods with nary a prayer on his lips to a more mature Christian who has seen those bushes afire with God. I've learned that we must first create a space of time, quiet, and isolation before we can truly see God. Three elements are necessary for this. We need to first believe, then learn to perceive, and finally receive.

Believe

To avoid a sentimental or idolatrous view of nature we need to first be fully converted to life in Christ. Martin Luther tells us, "Now if I believe in God's Son and bear in mind that He became man, all creatures will appear a hundred times more beautiful to me than before. Then I will properly appreciate the sun, the moon, the stars, trees, apples, pears, as I reflect that he is Lord over and the center of all things."[17] If we *don't* appreciate the out-of-doors, then maybe we don't appreciate the Creator.

Luther tells us that it is only with the "eye of faith" that we can see miracles all through nature, miracles that he believed were even greater than the miracles of the sacraments. If we truly understood the growth of a grain of wheat, he says, we would die of wonder.[18]

So the first way to become awakened is to seek the Creator behind the creation. Luther called creation the "mask of God." A mask partially conceals, but it also tells us that something is behind the mask.

Perceive

The second step to becoming awakened to God is to resurrect deadened elements of perception. Saint Bonaventure, another of Francis of Assisi's disciples, suggested a grid through which we may "school" ourselves to seek God out of doors.

First, consider the greatness of creation—mountains, sky, and oceans—that clearly portrays the immensity of the power, wisdom, and goodness of the triune God.

Next, look at the multitude of creation—a forest has more plant and animal life than you could examine in a lifetime and shows us how God is capable of doing many things at once. Those who wonder how God can hear so many prayers uttered simultaneously have been out of the forest too long.

Finally, examine the beauty of creation—see the beauty of rocks and their shapes, the beauty of colors and shades, the beauty of individual elements (like trees), and the beauty of overall composition (like forests). God's beauty cannot be revealed through one form, but is so vast and infinite it can fill an entire world with wonder.

> *Those who wonder how God can hear so many prayers uttered simultaneously have been out of the forest too long.*

The outdoors also speaks of God's abundance. We've talked much about the forest, but stand barefoot in a desert or on a beach and try to guess how many grains of sand are under your feet, or within your sight, or on all the beaches and deserts of the world. We serve a God of plenty, whose mercy and love are inexhaustible.[19]

When Graham, my son, was just two years old, we'd trek through the Manassas, Virginia, battlefield in silence. I'd occasionally point out a tree or a plant, and Graham would nod and move on. These were delightful walks for me since we were able to be together and still be reverent. Now that he's ten, it is virtually impossible for Graham and his friends to resist gathering pine cones and sticks to set up an "ambush" for the rest of the family as we walk by. He's not in the woods to perceive; he's in there to play—and there's a place for that.

For the true Christian naturalist, creation is nothing less than a sanctuary, a holy place that invites you to prayer. See how you can awaken your soul with creation. As you commute to work or the grocery store, consider driving a few extra blocks or even miles if it means you can pass through a country road. Take an extra moment to look around you and appreciate what God has made. Decide that traveling will be more important to you than reaching the next place. Make it an event.

Receive

Psychologists tell us that a child's fear of animals is frequently the result of transferring his or her own aggressions onto the beast. When we enter the woods, we can do the same; we transfer our own anxieties onto the scenery. Walks that are truly helpful are walks in which I lay down my agenda at the first sign of grass and let God lead my mind where he may.

I was headed down a wooded trail once, trying to solve a problem at work. My mind was preoccupied, but as I made my way farther down the trail, I sensed God correcting me. In a matter of yards my mind was clear and my heart was listening to God, loving him, being with him. The trail bent and began descending slightly. It was the beginning of spring, and a creek bed off Bull Run, which I had run across all winter, was now blocked by a freely flowing stream. I was stunned. That same, small path of earth I had easily crossed for several months was now under water. I had seen it like this before, but the suddenness of the change overwhelmed me and God's voice broke in: Opportunities change. If we don't cross when we can, we may not be able to cross at a later date.

> Walks that are truly helpful are walks in which I lay down my agenda at the first sign of grass and let God lead my mind where he may.

Thoughts, analogies, and ideas then flooded through my mind as I hiked around the creek bed to the small wooden footbridge that crossed it. There God planted new directions in my heart, and I lingered at that bridge, enjoying a rich time of worship. I reveled in the sight of the water running underneath me, the tree limbs catching leaves and small sticks, the sound of the water trickling, the smell of the clean air. I didn't want to leave. Yet I almost missed this blessing because my mind was so full when I entered the woods. God in his mercy broke in, and I left the woods deeply in love with a God who shares his heart and purposes with me.

We cannot receive, however, unless we set aside time for God to speak—and then let him set the agenda for our discussion. I've found that my agenda is frequently different from God's. He must be the initiator in my spiritual walk. He knows what I need to hear. When I'm consumed with my temporal problems, I miss the blessing of being out of doors.

When you come to the woods, come to receive. Leave your worries at home.

The Temptations of Naturalists

As with all the spiritual temperaments, naturalists have to be wary of some dangers.[20]

Individualism

Jesus spent time alone out of doors, but he did so in preparation for going back into the world. Even St. Francis stressed the need to leave his beloved countryside and enter the city to find souls who needed to hear about God. We must make sure we are not using creation to escape the duties of Christian living.

Spiritual Delusion

Psychologists have found that many people traveling through biblical lands become so overwhelmed they believe themselves to be a biblical character or even Christ himself. From the work of Henry David Thoreau to astronauts such as John Glenn, ample testimony has been given that there is something about creation that speaks powerfully into our souls. Sometimes God's voice whispers through nature; at other times, it practically screams.

We must remember, however, that such insights should be tested very carefully. Anything "received" on a walk with God should not be considered authoritative, but merely advice that must be tested. The Bible is the only sure guide, and we must guard against seeking an experience that Satan will only too gladly counterfeit in order to lead us astray.

Idolizing Nature

Some naturalists may tend to slip into the heresy of pantheism, which is a worship of nature. Pantheism is a lie. It is not true that God is in all of nature, or that nature is God. It is true, however, that every time I am surrounded by creation, I see that God is. The Bible teaches us that the earth is the Lord's. Pantheism twists this to say, "The earth is the Lord."[21] Pantheism has been enjoying a resurgence due to various New Age philosophies, and Christians are rightly concerned about incorporating such teachings into their worship. However, I am not going to allow the lie of pantheism to rob me of worshiping God through an appreciation of what he has made.

The distinction between pantheism and true Christian worship can be seen through an analogy of a mother missing a child who has recently left for college. The mother walks into her daughter's room, taking time to appreciate all that her daughter has left behind. She breathes in her daughter's pleasant scent, her eyes linger on the posters, the bed, a few clothes left behind. Her daughter isn't in the room, but the room reminds her that her daughter is. No doubt she feels closer to her daughter here than she would in any other part of the house. A part of her daughter has been left behind—not materially, but evidentially—in how her daughter has arranged the furniture, how she has decorated the walls, in the things she has collected.

> *It is not true that God is in all of nature, or that nature is God. It is true, however, that every time I am surrounded by creation, I see that God is.*

It is the same for a lover of God. God is not materially in nature, but his concern for detail, his overwhelming creativity, his orderliness, and much, much more are clearly present to the discerning eye. It can be intoxicating. Without the Holy Spirit we, too, might be led to cross the idolatrous line into pantheism. But with sound doctrine to instruct us and the Holy Spirit to guide us, we can appreciate nature's message that "God is" without falling into the heresy of pantheism.

Are You a Naturalist?

Are you a naturalist? At the end of each section describing the nine spiritual temperaments will be an exercise to help you determine if this temperament is a dominant one for you. Each time I will ask you to score a series of statements on a scale of five to one, with five being very true and one being not true at all. Record your answer in the space provided.

_____ 1. I feel closest to God when I'm surrounded by what he has made—the mountains, the forests, or the sea.

_____ 2. I feel cut off if I have to spend too much time indoors, just listening to speakers or singing songs. Nothing makes me feel closer to God than being outside.

_____ 3. I would prefer to worship God by spending an hour beside a small brook than by participating in a group service.

_____ 4. If I could escape to a garden to pray on a cold day, walk through a meadow on a warm day, and take a trip by myself to the mountains on another day, I would be very happy.

_____ 5. A book called Nature's Sanctuaries: A Picturebook would be appealing to me.

_____ 6. Seeing God's beauty in nature is more moving to me than understanding new concepts, participating in a formal religious service, or participating in social causes.

The total of all your answers. _____

The highest number of points possible is obviously thirty; the higher your score, the stronger the dominance of this spiritual temperament in your life. But remember most of us have more than one spiritual temperament. Any score of fifteen or higher indicates a tendency toward this temperament.

Please take a moment now to register this score in chapter eleven on page 217. Once you have reviewed all the spiritual temperaments and noted all your scores on this page, you will have a composite picture of your soul's path to God!

An Invitation

Some years ago I was putting on my shoes when my son came up to me and asked me where I was going. He knew it was too cold and wet for him to be outside, but he wanted to know where I was headed.

"The battlefield," I said.

"Why?" he asked.

I looked at him and touched his cheek. "I just pray a whole lot better out there."

As you can probably tell by this chapter, I have become a naturalist as my faith has deepened. I love to be in the middle of a deep forest or high on a mountain or out on the water. My schedule doesn't permit me to be out as much as I would like, but I have learned that there are few better places for me to earnestly seek God.

Once, while walking through a meadow and watching the sun go down, I realized that, regardless of personal pain, regardless of vocational frustration or success, regardless of financial excess or lack, if I could go out-of-doors, I'd always be a rich man.

Sometimes, though, nothing happens when I'm outside. I may not receive any new insights and God may not feel particularly close. This has taught me that the demand for spiritual experience can be as gluttonous as the desire for food, money, or sex. Desire for spiritual highs needs to be contained so that we can develop other parts of our being.

We'll be looking at eight other spiritual temperaments. Some of them have been great supplements to my journey as a naturalist; others I've learned about primarily through the experiences of other people. Christian experience is so vast that I'm thankful for the time God has given me on this earth (and promised me in heaven) to explore new and deeper ways to worship and love him more and more.

THREE

SENSATES: LOVING GOD WITH THE SENSES

Henri Nouwen, a priest and prolific writer on the spiritual life, had just finished an exhausting lecture tour and was "dead tired, so much so that I could barely walk." He was anxious, lonely, restless, and, in his words, "very needy." As he visited the office of a friend, he came across a reproduction of Rembrandt's *The Return of the Prodigal Son*. Stunned by the painting's power and beauty, Nouwen told his friend, "It's beautiful, more than beautiful . . . it makes me want to cry and laugh at the same time . . . I can't tell you what I feel as I look at it, but it touches me deeply."[1]

Nouwen writes:

> Rembrandt's embrace remained imprinted on my soul far more profoundly than any temporary expression of emotional support. It had brought me into touch with something within me that lies far beyond the ups and downs of a busy life, something that represents the ongoing yearning of the

human spirit.... The yearning for a lasting home, brought to consciousness by Rembrandt's painting, grew deeper and stronger, somehow making the painter himself into a faithful companion and guide. This seemingly insignificant encounter with one of Rembrandt's masterpieces set in motion a long spiritual adventure that brought me to a new understanding of my vocation and offered me new strength to live it.[2]

God used this painting to confirm Nouwen's call to minister in a community for mentally disabled adults. The power of art to move us into a deeper understanding of God's truth and nature has been grossly neglected by some in the Christian community. Throughout the ages, the most magnificent art has been produced in the name of faith.

As I've lived and studied the Christian life, I've found that some Christians are moved more by a sensuous worship experience than by anything else. By sensuous I'm referring to the five senses: taste, touch, smell, sound, and sight. When we reduce all Christian worship to mere intellectual assent, we force Christians to worship God in a crippled existence. When we embrace the use of the senses—which God created, after all—we open up entirely new avenues of worship.

> *Biblical accounts of the glory of God in heaven are elaborate affairs and rarely quiet, to say the least.*

This may be a difficult message for Christians who grew up, as I did, equating silence and lack of sensory stimulation with reverence. When we look at Scripture, however, we find that God often appears in a very loud and colorful way.

The Loud and Colorful God of Scripture

Biblical accounts of the glory of God in heaven are elaborate affairs and rarely quiet, to say the least. Consider, for example, the experience recounted by Ezekiel. He *feels* a wind. He *sees* flashing lightning surrounded by brilliant light, fantastic creatures, and a magnificent and stunning throne of sapphire.[3] He *hears* the sound of wings like the roar of rushing waters, and a loud rumbling.[4] Ezekiel is then asked to *eat* a scroll that tastes sweet. After it is all over, Ezekiel is so overwhelmed—perhaps the sensuous onslaught is so great—he sits down, stunned, for seven days.[5]

A similar appearance occurs in Ezekiel, chapter 10, where Ezekiel experiences burning coals, great radiance, a loud sound, clouds filling the temple, and fantastic sights and movements—wheels that sparkled like chrysolite, and cherubim with four faces.

When the Glory returns to the temple, we again read that God's voice is like the "roar of rushing waters"[6] and the land becomes radiant with his glory. The sight is so great that Ezekiel falls facedown.

When Christ appears to John in the book of Revelation, the experience is also a very sensuous one. When Jesus proclaims his name, John describes it as a "loud voice like a trumpet." Jesus' head and hair were "white like wool . . . and his eyes were like blazing fire." Jesus' voice was "like the sound of rushing waters." Jesus'

> *There is something within each of us that is awed by the presence of beauty.*

face "was like the sun shining in all its brilliance." As anybody who tries to look into the sun knows, such brilliance forces you to turn away, and that's what happened to John. "I fell at his feet as though dead."[7]

These pictures of God in his glory contrast greatly with the calm, quiet, "greeting-card" Jesus often depicted today. And they bear absolutely no resemblance to a bruised and bleeding Jesus suffering on a cross. Those who think only silence is reverent may be a bit uncomfortable in heaven, and this is the lesson we learn from the sensate.

To be honest, the sensate is one of the more difficult temperaments for me. I much prefer the out-of-doors or quiet solitude to overwhelming stimulation. Yet there is something within me, within each of us, that is awed by the presence of beauty. I believe it's a flashing glimpse of our desire for the transcendence of heaven. Looking at it this way, I could at least be open to the sensuous side of worship.

The Benefit of a Sense of Beauty

Von Ogden Vogt, a pastor in the early part of this century, described parallels between our contact with beauty and with God; these parallels, I think, will help us to better appreciate the role of the sensate.[8] First, beauty arouses *humility*. You go to the opera, for instance, and say, "I could never write an opera like that if I lived a thousand years." I remember early in college wanting to be a fiction writer and almost throwing a book by Charles Dickens down in frustration; the writing was so good, it humiliated my own efforts. This humiliation is necessary. Once we've experienced such quality, we can never go back to the mediocre; just as once we have tasted God, we lose our taste for the world.

The second step, according to Vogt, moves us from humiliation to *dignity*. We recognize we may not be able to write such an opera, but there are other things we can do. Once we are truly humbled, God enlightens us as to what we can do, and this gives us a new sense of dignity.

The third stage produces *a different worldview*. "The unworthy sinks, the true and the good emerge and grow." Parents sometimes witness this transformation when their rock-and-roll-listening, comic-book-reading child comes home from college listening to classical music and talking about the latest book by M. Scott Peck.

The fourth and final stage results in *a recognition* that we must return to the real world. You can't stay in the theater or museum forever; worship in church must give way to evangelism on the streets. But we're different persons from having encountered beauty or God.

There are limits to the analogy, of course. Beauty doesn't result in improved morality, whereas interaction with God does, or at least, should. The search for beauty can be selfish, whereas God calls us to die to ourselves. But the four stages of beauty do mirror Isaiah's call to repentance, cleansing, illumination, and enlistment.[9] Christianity without beauty becomes a disembodied religion of the mind. Truth—thought—is an essential component of real Christianity. But feeling is also important, for we are told to love God not only with all our mind, but our heart as well. Furthermore, truth as a concept is often not enough for people who live in the world of senses. Vogt writes:

Truth must be embodied to be realized. It must be incorporated to be understood. No religious movement has ever been forceful or popular without a rich corporeality. An image, a rite, a creed, a feeling, a feast, a vision, or a sacrament has always been used to embody its truth.[10]

Vogt admits that we need the prophets who preach against idolatry and sensuous abuse; but he also maintains that people haven't been able to understand truth without a symbol, sacrament, or rite in which they can express that truth. That's where beauty comes in; anything that is going to express the truth of heaven must be as beautiful as is humanly possible.

Awakening the Senses

I was very glad to be sitting alone when I received Communion at Regent College's chapel service for the first time; otherwise, I would surely have embarrassed myself. The bread was passed; a familiar experience. Next, the cup came around. I opened my mouth, drank, and for the first time in my life, tasted red wine.

I grew up Baptist, which meant we celebrated the Lord's Supper with grape juice or even Kool-aid (I'm not kidding!), depending on who drew Communion service that month. The wine caught me totally by surprise. I won't try to describe the look on my face, but I'm glad that nobody saw it. As I left the chapel service, I noticed that the taste of the wine was still with me. Its taste kept reminding me of the truth of Communion for hours afterward. That was perhaps one of the first experiences I had of the benefits of vivid sensory experience in worship.

As I hinted earlier, I'm not a very sensuous person; musically, my tastes are very unschooled and immature. I can fully relate to theologian Carl F. H. Henry, who said he was looking forward to heaven because then he'd be able to sing the great hymns with more than one note. Incense, to be honest, is usually distasteful to me. Elaborate architecture is beautiful to visit as a tourist, but I sometimes find it a distraction (rather than an invitation) to true worship.

I need to remember, though, that God created our senses. Enjoyment through the senses was his idea, not Satan's. Let's look at some of the ways the senses have been used in Christian worship.

Sound

For those who believe that the quieter a building is, the more holy the environment, using sound to love God might sound paradoxical. Certainly, there is a great need for times of silence, but there is also a great tradition of sound being used to serve God, and that tradition starts in the Bible. We've already mentioned the rather loud appearances of God to Ezekiel and John. There is much more. Psalm 96 begins with, "Sing to the LORD a new song; sing to the LORD, all the earth. Sing to the LORD, praise his name." Psalms 147, 149, and 150 urge believers to worship God through making music on instruments.[11]

In a very real sense, the congregation may be more "alive" during special music than during the sermon. And they may remember the verses long after they've forgotten the teaching.

Scripture's admonition to use music in worship shouldn't surprise us. As our Creator, God knows that language and music together stimulate the brain more than just language on its own; in a very real sense, the congregation may be more "alive" during special music than during the sermon. And they may remember the verses long after they've forgotten the teaching.

Beautiful music has been a part of church life since its beginning. The great composer Handel recognized what he called the "transcendental keys." Any key signature with five, six, seven, or eight sharps he associated with heaven. He used particular chords to bring forth various feelings—G minor, to evoke urgency or jealousy; E minor, to create a sorrowful, lamenting mood; G major, to create moods reminiscent of bright sunlight and green pastures; F minor, to provoke gloom and despondency.[12]

It's interesting to note that Luther argued that Scripture was meant to be heard more than read. Our hearts are most transformed and challenged, he thought, when we hear the Word of God. Science has proven the validity of Luther's insight. When we hear Scripture read, our minds are more active than when we're just reading.

Smell

What does church smell like? Many Protestants would consider this an absurd question. Other traditions, however, would immediately try to convey the use of incense.

Smell can cement memories. When I smell Johnson's baby shampoo, I remember giving baths to my children; a certain of my wife's perfumes evokes memories of our date nights.

Perhaps it is this property of smell that caused incense to play such a key role in Old Testament worship. The familiar smell can remind the worshiper of a time when worship may have been particularly rich. After the service, lingering scents remind the believer of the worship experience. After a while the smell can condition the believer to consciously enter into the presence of God.

God commanded Moses to collect offerings of spices to create sweet incense.[13] Aaron was told that he must burn incense every morning.[14] Eli and Solomon both kept the practice of burning incense alive. Detailed instructions for cultivating sweet smells is given in Exodus 30.

God prophesies in Malachi that "from the rising to the setting of the sun . . . in every place incense and pure offerings will be brought to my name."[15] Frankincense was one of the offerings presented to the Christ child.[16] John the Baptist's father, Zacharias, was burning incense when the angel appeared to him and told him that his wife would conceive and give birth.[17] Incense continues to be offered to God in heaven, along with the prayers of the saints, according to the book of Revelation. Psalm 141:2 mentions that incense symbolizes prayers rising to God.

Negative examples of offering incense also occur in the Bible, but these are connected to idol worship[18] or offered in the context of a lapsed faith.[19] The abuse of incense is rejected, not its use.

There is no Eastern Orthodox corporate worship without incense. While some Lutheran and Episcopalian churches might employ incense, it's not likely you'll find it in a Presbyterian church, and certainly not in a Baptist one. Still, if an individual believer is having difficulty making a transition into prayer, he or she might find that incorporating a familiar smell could help.

The use of incense has not been, of course, without its critics. Even putting aside some of the reformers, who were frequently violently opposed to incense, some early Christians had their misgivings as well. Basil the Great, for instance, wrote, "Incense is now an abomination unto the Lord. For truly it is an execrable thing to think that God values the pleasures of the sense of smell and not to understand that the hallowing of the body, effected by the sobriety of the soul, is the incense unto the Lord. Corporeal incense that affects the nostrils and moves the sense is by a necessary consequence regarded as an abomination to a Being that is incorporeal."[20]

Basil is right in insisting that God couldn't care less about our burning incense as a sacrifice for our transgressions. No incense offering today will wipe out a single sin. However, incense isn't used to court favor with God, but to help the Christian pray. It is a means, not an end.

Physiologically our minds are sharpened and altered in the presence of incense.[21] This is not to make the use of incense obligatory; some Christians may be distracted by strong smells. But just because something isn't an effective worship aid for some doesn't mean other Christians can't enjoy it for themselves.

It's interesting to me that many Christians who reject incense wear perfume or cologne for very unspiritual reasons. Or they may use a car deodorizer, or choose a particular shampoo because of the way it smells. If smell can be used to welcome our guests or provide a special treat for our spouse, why can't it be used as an aid to worship? The use of smell in the one context and the rejection of it in the other is an arbitrary and artificial distinction.

Because some very helpful activities in the history of the church (i.e., walking the stations of the cross, using incense, and other such activities) have occasionally become polluted or separated from a vibrant faith, some Christians have thrown most of them away. We have cut too far, however, amputating the arm because we fear an infection in the finger.

The elements that hint at a transcendent reality that we have allowed to remain are surprisingly few: preaching, Bible study, prayer, a symbolic representation of the Lord's supper, and singing songs. As evangelical Christians we've confined ourselves to one tiny corner of the room, rather than living in a vast museum of spiritual opportunity.

Touch

A frequent complaint I hear from Christians is that they find it hard to stay awake and/or focused during prayer, especially in the early morning.

These Christians might find prayer easier if they assembled small objects to hold in their hands as they prayed for various people. A paper clip could help them focus on a marriage that is falling apart; a rubber band could help them pray for a pliable heart.

One Easter season I carried a nail in my pocket, reminding me to pray prayers of intercession and repentance throughout the Easter season. The sharp edge reminded me of Christ's sufferings every time I touched it or bent over and felt it pressing into my leg. Touch communicates, especially to the sensate Christian.

Because some very helpful activities in the history of the church ... have occasionally become polluted ... some Christians have thrown most of them away. We have cut too far, however, amputating the arm because we fear an infection in the finger.

Orthodox worship involves frequent kissing—a cross, an altar, a holy instrument. Touch with our lips is a way to recognize something as precious. It makes a powerful inner statement as well as an outward one. Once when I was in our attic I pulled out of a box some clothes that our oldest daughter had worn as an infant. I was flooded with rich memories of that special time and without thinking held one garment to my face and kissed it.

I don't apologize for being somewhat sentimental about my children; how much less should I apologize for being moved by the reality of the cross. Where, indeed, would I be without the cross? Given this, what can be wrong with a spontaneous (or not so spontaneous) kiss?

One of my most memorable times of prayer occurred spontaneously. I was a young college student and wanted to offer everything I had to God. Without really thinking about it, I offered God myself by touching various parts of my body. First I touched my fingers and feet, praying that God would consecrate them for his service. "Whenever I reach out, I want to reach out in love. Wherever I travel, I want to do so under Christ's name." Next I touched my lips. "Whatever I speak, let it be the truth and something that will bring glory to your kingdom." I touched my eyes. "Help me to protect my eyes, only letting them see what is helpful for the inner man within, so that my 'inner eye' will not be blind to the sight of the real needs around me." On I went, offering up the various parts of my body for God's service.

> *[Nouwen] had read the story of the prodigal son innumerable times before. Yet once his soul was captivated by Rembrandt's work, the truth of that parable pierced Nouwen's heart with an entirely new passion.*

Later, my wife pointed out that I had gone through motions similar to blood consecration in Leviticus 8:24 where Moses sprinkles blood on Aaron's sons, placing it on the tips of their right ears, the thumbs of their right hands, and the big toes of their right feet.

I didn't plan this prayer beforehand; it just happened. I don't know how many times I've prayed, but most of them have been forgotten; yet this prayer has remained with me.

Sight

Henri Nouwen had lectured at Yale for several years before he was moved so profoundly by Rembrandt's *The Return of the Prodigal Son.* There were probably very few theological points or arguments

Nouwen hadn't studied several times over. Certainly, he had read the story of the prodigal son innumerable times before. Yet once his soul was captivated by Rembrandt's work, the truth of that parable pierced Nouwen's heart with an entirely new passion.

"I felt drawn by the intimacy between the two figures, the warm red of the man's cloak, the golden yellow of the boy's tunic, and the mysterious light engulfing them both. But, most of all, it was the hands, the old man's hands, as they touched the boy's shoulders that reached me in a place where I had never been reached before."[22]

Sight affects us perhaps more than any other sense. As much as a third of our cerebral cortex, which is the highest level of our brain, is devoted to visual processing. Researchers have even found that sight can be used to affect our will, which has a direct bearing on our commitment to live out our faith.

Journalist Michael Long writes, "In a profound and mysterious alchemy, sight sometimes combines with memory to energize the will. After his return from more than six years of captivity in Lebanon, American hostage Thomas Sutherland related that he had tried to commit suicide three times, but that each time, 'the vision of my wife and three daughters appeared before me' and he could not follow through."[23]

The use of sight in Christian worship and prayer is rooted in the incarnation, though sight was also an integral element of Old Testament worship. When God inaugurated Israel's form of worship, he especially gifted and called out two individuals, Bezalel and Oholiab, to do "all kinds of crafts."[24] These workers created beautiful art forms out of gold, silver, bronze, and wood. They also developed skill in embroidering fine linen and making intricate and fashionable weaves.

The sight of the finished temple must have taken the worshipers' breath away. To God, beauty mattered. The expense of the temple was an acceptable sacrifice, and those who used their gifts to build it were held in high esteem and said to be "filled with the Spirit of God."

It's true that Jesus told the woman at the well that worship must be done in spirit and truth, but he was confronting the misconception that worship should be limited to one particular place. On another occasion, Jesus himself accepted lavish worship: the offering of expensive, sweet-smelling perfume.

I've been in a number of churches that were just starting out, so I know from experience that you can truly worship God just about anywhere, including a high school cafeteria with a flashing red digital sign overhead! However, the fact that we can worship in such surroundings doesn't mean we should if the opportunity presents itself to find more appropriate accommodations.

"The average church interior is uninteresting," says Pastor Von Ogden Vogt. "Without necessarily being ugly in detail, there is no commanding excellence. . . . Your building will have an effect whether you want it to or not, and this effect of ineffectiveness is one of the most unfortunate." He warns against creating a building that is either overly comfortable or cold and dreary.[25]

Ironically, building committees are rarely chosen with regard to a person's architectural insight. Most of us lack the training to be able to appreciate the various elements in Greek, Roman, Byzantine, Romanesque, Gothic, or Renaissance architecture and apply them to today.

I am certainly no student of architecture, but like anyone, I am affected by the general "tone" of a certain room, knowing whether it makes me peaceful or restless. Great architects of the faith were able to merge positive tones such as repose (symbolic of the sufficiency of religion), harmony and peace, austerity (calls for mortification of the flesh), warmth, and brilliance.[26] It takes a great architect to pull off such a feat, let alone a building committee consisting of a lawyer, two home-makers, a banker, a schoolteacher, an engineer, and a pastor.

Some people may not be bothered by a room surrounded by signs announcing the upcoming prom, yearbook sale, and pep rally; and yet the sensate Christian would feel assaulted. It is naive, however, to ignore the fact that our surroundings affect all of us to a greater or lesser degree. Cathedrals were constructed as a call to worship, so that our thoughts would be pulled heavenward when we entered them.

Besides worship rooms, other Christians have made use of sight through pictures or icons. The sight of an icon, symbolizing a saint's obe-dience, might help an Orthodox Christian finally say "Yes" to a hard word from Scripture. At another time the image presented by the icon may help lead the Christian into prayer. Praying to an icon is never an acceptable form of worship, but the true Christian may be helped to focus by being reminded of the reality that the icon represents.

It might make sense to encourage children to close their eyes so they can focus on prayer since children are easily distracted. But as we mature, we may find that looking at someone (or a picture of someone) while we pray for them increases our ability to pray. We may find that looking into the heavens as we worship, pray, or recite a psalm adds to the sincerity of our words rather than getting in the way. Certainly, since sight affects us so greatly, we would do well to incorporate it into our worship.

Since sight affects us so greatly, we would do well to incorporate it into our worship.

Sensates might also find that drawing can be a great aid to prayer. The following is an exercise suggested by a Christian group based in London:

A. Draw a representation of what God means to you. Then depict yourself in relationship to God in whatever manner seems appropriate to you. Note: stick figures and simple symbolism will suffice; this needn't be a professional work of art!

B. On another sheet of paper or by altering your first drawing, depict how you *wish* God might be for you and how you *wish* you could be in relationship with God.

C. Draw onto either sheet the things which seem to get in the way of God being for you as you would wish.

D. Pray your pictures in silence in whatever way is helpful to you.[27]

Creative Christians can find their own ways to incorporate the element of sight into prayer.

Taste

Taste affects us so greatly, we use it to describe many things. A cultured person, we say, has "good taste." A crude or vulgar person "lacks taste." A cranky or vengeful person is "bitter." Someone very kind is "sweet." Getting a new job that calls us to relocate can be called "bittersweet." Two researchers have said, "It seems that the perceptions that we call taste are so powerful, so extensive in their capacity to conjure up clusters of associated feelings, that we freely transfer the language of taste to all other parts of our experience."[28]

If this is so, why can't we use taste to benefit our spiritual lives? I've already mentioned how real wine affected my experience at Communion. We must be careful that the sensory side of Communion doesn't deter us from the commitment Communion calls us to; but for a healthy soul, taste can reinforce the Communion experience, especially if we take our time and don't rush right through it.

Taste can also be used in our prayers. Something sweet can remind us of God's goodness; something bitter can keep us praying for a seemingly unanswered prayer. Most of us eat two or three meals a day; some of us also enjoy a few snacks in between meals. If we condition ourselves to relate taste to worship, we can be reminded to worship several times a day.

Certain scriptural passages lend themselves to taste. Matthew 7:16 tells us we can know a person by his or her fruits; think about this the next time you bite into a particularly delicious (or rotten) apple or orange. Jesus describes himself as the bread of life; he calls us the salt of the earth. As we study these passages, or as we are reminded of them in everyday life, we can incorporate spiritual awakening into the otherwise routine act of eating.

God created taste; it was his idea. If we're creative, we can find ways to love him through it.

The Temptations of Sensates

Despite the many benefits we might experience through using our senses to worship God, there are also many dangers. Sensate Christians in particular need to be aware of these:

Worshiping Without Conviction

Senses can deceive, especially when our emotions are sent soaring through music. In college, we had a number of concerts with well-known Christian artists. Some artists used the music to convey a clear message. Other performers focused solely on the music. In some cases this would be fine—entertainment has its place—but in the midst of this event an altar call was given. People were very worked up after a particular song, and many went forward. A few days later one of the women who had made a "decision" told my

> *Words may be sung with scarcely more emotion than I feel when I'm ordering a hamburger.*

wife, "The music just got me in the mood. I didn't really mean it." Her faith died before the amplifiers had cooled off.

The same thing can happen to us when we worship. It amazes me how casually I can sing songs of deep, almost heroic commitment. It's as if I think, *As long as I'm singing, the words I say don't really matter. God knows it's just a song.* While my mind wanders I promise to bow before the Lord, to proclaim his name to the ends of the earth, and to go so far as to die to express my faith. Yet these words may be sung with scarcely more emotion than I feel when I'm ordering a hamburger. How often do we Christians "take the Lord's name in vain" during our worship?

It matters to God if we lie, even if we're singing, and even if everybody around us is singing the same thing. Music can make us feign a commitment that just isn't there, causing us to become callous, insincere believers.

Idolizing Beauty

Just as naturalists can fall into idolatry if they let eros slip into an appreciation for creation, so the sensate Christian can slip into idolatry if eros enters the appreciation of an elaborate cathedral or a beautifully painted icon.

When God's servants, mere angels, appeared to people in the Bible, even mature prophets were tempted to worship them. Things of great beauty can steal our heart from the only One worthy of true, unadulterated worship. Somebody might leave a very beautiful liturgical service satisfied by the sensuous experience without having entered the true presence of God.

Worshiping Worship

Unfortunately we can mistakenly slip from using our senses to worship God, to using our senses to worship worship. Many of the great Christian classics warn that sensuous worship is immature, or at least inferior to the dark night of the faith favored by contemplatives. I don't fully subscribe to this view, but I do believe that the senses can be very misleading, especially if we confuse sensory stimulation with a true commitment of the will.

On the other hand, using sensory stimulation as an aid to worship doesn't necessarily mean that the Christian is dependent upon it or would be lost without it; I can get by on one meal a day, but I'd prefer not to. And we can't deny that some Christians really do find sensuous aids to be a help in their faith.

Are You a Sensate?

Are you a sensate? As in chapter two, score the following statements on a scale of five to one, with five being very true and one being not true at all. Record your answer in the space before the paragraph:

_____ 1. I feel closest to God when I'm in a church that allows my senses to come alive—when I can see, smell, hear, and almost taste his majesty.

_____ 2. I enjoy attending a "high church" service with incense and formal Communion or Eucharist.

_____ 3. I'd have a difficult time worshiping in a church building that is plain and lacks a sense of awe or majesty. Beauty is very important to me, and I have a difficult time worshiping through second-rate Christian art or music.

_____ 4. The words *sensuous, colorful,* and *aromatic* are very appealing to me.

_____ 5. A book called *The Beauty of Worship* would be appealing to me.

_____ 6. I would really enjoy using drawing exercises or art to improve my prayer life.

The total of all your answers. _____

Again the highest number of points possible is thirty, but few, if any, will score that high since none of us relate to God in one exclusive way. Any score of fifteen or higher indicates a tendency toward this spiritual temperament.

Please take a moment now to register this score in chapter eleven on page 217. Once you have reviewed all the spiritual temperaments and noted all your scores on this page, you will have a composite picture of your soul's path to God.

An Invitation to Beautiful Worship

Von Ogden Vogt, the pastor from the early part of this century, issued a call to churches that provides an appropriate closing for this chapter on sensate Christians:

Quietly and naturally we can improve our ordinary public worship in many ways, by simpler, nobler, and more beautiful church buildings; by altogether more pertinent and disposed religious music; by high points of stimulus in the placing of a painting, a window . . .; by a more unified and climactic order of service; by patient attention at many little points in the administration of the sacraments; by better prepared prayers; and by more instruction for securing spiritual effort and reverent expectancy on the part of the people.[29]

> *Using our bodies to glorify God is a much better response than denying the role of the body in worship.*

Remember, sight, sound, taste, touch, and smell are God's gifts more than they are Satan's temptations. Using our bodies to glorify God is a much better response than denying the role of the body in worship, and then turning around and using the body in areas that lead to sin. Gnosticism, emphasizing a special knowledge, and therefore making the mind the only arena that really matters, was discarded as a heresy centuries ago.

When I die, I hope that I will have been able to love God with everything I am: I will have worked to turn my mind over to his wisdom and truth, my hands over to his service, my sight over to his beauty, and my entire being over to enjoying his presence.

FOUR

TRADITIONALISTS: LOVING GOD THROUGH RITUAL AND SYMBOL

That didn't take long," I said to myself as I stood up from the old wooden pew and made my way to the side door of the church, up near the altar. "These Episcopalians sure know how to hold a short service."

The priest turned and saw me walk up the aisle. A distinctly puzzled look covered his face. I glanced sideways and realized to my horror that people were sitting down, not leaving. The service wasn't over at all, it was just beginning.

With a face redder than the wine that was served for Communion, I slunk down into the closest available pew. "Passing the peace," I learned, wasn't a benediction, it was like the Baptist "Please shake everybody's hand."

The experience was all the more embarrassing because I was not a new Christian when it occurred. I had attended thousands of church services. I was raised in a Baptist church, however, and during college and seminary I attended what was basically an interdenominational church. This was my first liturgical service, and I felt as ill at ease as when my college missions group attended a Sikh wedding to get a cross-cultural experience.

If you weren't raised in a liturgical setting, it takes a while to get used to it, but the benefits can be tremendous, even for someone raised a Baptist. Sometimes, just stepping out of our tradition will help us understand familiar parts of the faith in a new way. Listen to what a Presbyterian poet and writer, Kathleen Norris, said:

> I think I'm typical of a lot of people in my generation. I simply stopped going to church after high school. I really can't explain what it was that ten years later drew me back. Ironically, I think it was the Benedictines that kept me at it. I'm married. I'm not a Catholic. But when I started attending their liturgy, they would sing or recite psalms, have a Bible reading, and some prayers four times a day. Being able to say and hear poems out loud was a whole new approach for me, even though it's about 1,700 years old. It really nourished me and made me a better Presbyterian.[1]

Kathleen now describes herself as a "Presbyterian Benedictine." I think she speaks for many Christians who want to remain in their tradition, but have found some elements of worship in other Christian traditions that greatly increase their faith.

Some people react to the word *religion* like a child reacts to the word *bedtime*. They rightly fear a form of faith that has no substance so they stress, "Christianity is a relationship, not a religion."

However, in the context of a true faith, religious practices and rituals can be a powerful force for good—a friend, not an enemy, of a rich and growing relationship with God.

The Biblical Account of Religious Practices

For all our suspicion of religious practices, we must remember that God invented (and at times commanded) much of them; they marked the lives of the Old Testament patriarchs. Furthermore, even the New Testament champions of "salvation by grace through faith" were eager practitioners of certain religious practices—not to earn salvation, certainly, but to nourish their faith.

Religious practices are the way men and women embody spiritual truths. Thus the Bible contains a rich tradition of "sanctified religious practices."

Abraham expressed his faith by building altars. When God appeared to him at Shechem and told Abraham that the Canaanites' land would one day be his, Abraham built an altar to the Lord. When he moved from there and pitched his tent between Bethel and Ai, Abraham built another altar to the Lord. Abraham followed the same practice when he moved to Hebron. By doing this, Abraham sought to bring form to his faith.[2]

Even the New Testament champions of "salvation by grace through faith" were eager practitioners of certain religious practices—not to earn salvation, certainly, but to nourish their faith.

When God began to formalize Israel's religion, he rejected idol worship and instead commanded that Moses make an altar of earth for burnt offerings. God was reorienting religious practices, not rejecting them. In fact Aaron and his sons were given elaborate religious rituals to follow,[3] which would "distinguish between the holy and the common,"[4] so that reverence for God wouldn't be lost.

Modern Christians might scoff at such symbolism. "That stuff was for the unenlightened and the superstitious," we might say. "Surely God doesn't really care about such symbolism." But he does care—at the very least, he did care very much—for when Nadab and Abihu, two of Aaron's sons, "offered unauthorized fire before the LORD," God took their lives. After Nadab and Abihu's deaths God gave more specific instructions to Moses about how priests were to come into his presence.[5]

God understands that our reaction to symbols often reveals our hearts' reaction to him. If we're flippant toward symbols, we're often flippant toward what the symbols represent. Wanting to guard against this, God instructed Moses to follow the exact pattern God gave him when he constructed the tabernacle.[6] Moses was told not to depart from this.

Ezra was also a traditionalist. He studied the law and taught its decrees; proclaimed fasts; offered sacrifices; mourned over sin; made confessions; and publicly read the law.[7]

Many New Testament figures observed religious rituals as well, teaching us that religion still has a place in our worship, even though the substance of Christianity is based on faith. Jesus' custom was to go to the synagogue on the Sabbath. (If Jesus saw the need for regular, formal worship, how much more so should we!) Peter and John both observed regular, set times of prayer. Paul, the champion of receiving salvation by grace through faith, nevertheless observed the religious custom in Philippi of praying by the riverside on the Sabbath. He also willingly underwent the ritual of purification.[8]

> *These New Testament figures made it clear that no one will be saved through religion alone; but they also made it clear, by their example, that Christians can be nourished by certain religious practices.*

These New Testament figures made it clear that no one will be saved through religion alone; but they also made it clear, by their example, that Christians can be nourished by certain religious practices.

Elements of Traditionalist Expression of Faith

I think I'll always remember my first walk into the National Cathedral in Washington, D.C. The churches of my childhood were usually long buildings with a cross in the front. If you removed the cross and put down a rubber floor, you'd have a gymnasium.

The Cathedral was altogether different. "It's a castle!" my daughter, Allison, shouted the first time we drove by.

The doors were heavy and solid. The stones in the floor and steps gave me a secure feeling, like I was walking on a foundation no less sturdy than the earth itself. When I first walked into the main sanctuary, I felt small, much smaller even than when I gazed into the sky. There are side chapels, some with candles flickering, and halls containing the crypts of Christians who died long ago. My eyes rested on the Canterbury pulpit, so majestic that it almost made me laugh when I thought of the music stands I had preached behind.

I found that prayer services were held at noon. Later, I'd try to catch one or two, or spend an afternoon praying in one of the side chapels. Praying became difficult, however; the National Cathedral is a tourist attraction as much as a sanctuary, and you soon find that any type of prolonged solitude is impossible.

My wife was somewhat surprised by my interest in this religious building. Earlier in my life, my Christianity was lived out on the streets witnessing to nonbelievers and taking a stand for justice. It was a new thing to see me tucked away in a cathedral, seeking to pray to God surrounded by religious trappings.

The same elements that some have discarded as lifeless—because in their childhood they were removed from a real expression of faith—began to nourish my soul in new ways and create a strength and depth in my spiritual life that had been missing. Those experiences have given me a new appreciation for the traditionalist temperament.

There are three elements of the traditionalist pathway:

- ritual (or liturgical pattern);
- symbol (or significant image);
- and sacrifice.

Evelyn Underhill, a popular Christian writer in the early part of this century, calls these three elements "sensible signs of supra-sensible action."[9] They are ways we use the physical world to express nonphysical (spiritual) truths.

Ritual

The power of rites is quite simply the power of reinforced behavior. Protestants, Roman Catholics, and Eastern Orthodox Christians may disagree about which rituals are most appropriate, but all Christians can benefit by them.

Gertrud Mueller Nelson, a contemporary writer and artist, says, "God proceeded to create a world of order with space, matter, time, life, and humans in his own image. Through ritual and ceremonies we people in turn make order out of chaos. In endless space, we create a fixed point to orient ourselves: a sacred space. To timelessness we impose rhythmic repetitions: the recurrent feast. . . . What is too vast and shapeless, we deal with in smaller, manageable pieces. We do this for practicality but we also do this for high purpose: to relate safely to the mysterious, to communicate with the transcendent."[10]

To explain further, she mentions a practice we have all seen. Watch how children, frightened by the vast and powerful surf at the ocean, "tame" it; they scoop a small hole in the sand near where the waves break and let the water fill the hole. In essence, children respond to the vast sea by creating a "mini-sea," which they can control and manage. "They had created a hole," Nelson writes, "to catch something of the transcendent. In the same way we cannot head straight into the awe of the Almighty. Like the child before the ocean, we turn our backs on what is too much and slowly create the form that will contain something of the uncontainable. . . . The power of the Almighty needs, sometimes, to be guarded against but it also needs to be beckoned, called forth, and wooed."[11]

Rituals, like sacraments, provide a way for us to enter into God's glory and still be protected from a force that is too great for human experience. Let's review some of these rituals.

Celebrations and Observances

My daughter wouldn't let go of my hand. I could sense her insecurity and bent down to talk to her.

"What's up?" I asked.

"I'm so fancy," she said, touching her dress, embarrassed.

I looked around. We were surrounded by people wearing leather coats, colored T-shirts, shiny jackets with professional sports logos on them, blue jeans—the standard crowd in a jail waiting room. Allison and I had just come from a Good Friday children's service, and we were waiting to visit an inmate.

"That's all right," I told her. "It's Good Friday. They'll just figure you've been to church."

After an unusually long wait, the inmate's name was called, and we made our way into the cell blocks. I had prepared Allison for what she would see—the man we were visiting would be in a glass-enclosed room, and we'd have to talk through a phone. Finally we found him and began talking.

"It took a long time," I said.

"I was in the gym," he answered.

"Are they going to be doing anything inside for Easter?" I asked after some time.

"Is it Easter this weekend?" he asked. "I thought that was last weekend. Jesus of Nazareth was on television, so I thought it must have been Easter."

I have to confess, my heart sank a bit. I'm not particularly pious when it comes to these things, but the thought of another believer playing basketball on Good Friday without knowing that Easter was around the corner saddened me.

This person has a hard time submitting his life to Christ. The desire is there, but pressures arise and he sometimes falters. A good, four-day celebration like Easter could do wonders.

At certain points in church history, Easter was a *forty-day celebration*. Forty days is too much for our busy culture, so we've shortened it to four—Maundy Thursday, Good Friday, Holy Saturday, and Easter Sunday. But even this is becoming too much for the modern Christian, so we watch *The Robe* on Saturday night and show up, fresh and pretty, on Sunday morning.

It doesn't have to be this way. Religious observances have their place. They can be lifeless rituals or life-altering encounters, depending upon how we approach them. If we're willing to step back from the world for a few days, we might find that God can fill our celebrations with a power we never knew existed.

Walter Wangerin did the church a great service when he wrote *Reliving the Passion*.[12] Wangerin's little book provides a short meditation, based on the Gospel of Mark, that takes the reader from Ash Wednesday to Easter Sunday. Tricia Rhodes has written a similar book entitled *Contemplating the Cross*. Other books have been written to help Christians

> *Religious observances ...
> can be lifeless rituals or life-altering encounters,
> depending upon how we
> approach them.*

celebrate Christmas. While some Christians argue that we should ignore these observances, traditionalists will say, with good reason, that we ought to out-celebrate everyone.

A mother who goes out of her way to make Christmas and Easter special is doing her family an exemplary Christian service. A father who explains what certain Sundays and celebrations mean is doing a tremendous pastoral work for his children.

It is all the more important to do this in a culture that is increasingly post-Christian. My wife and I were awakened to this need when we took a new Christian to his first Christmas Eve service. As we pulled up to the church he asked, "I understand why we celebrate Christmas, but isn't Christ's death and resurrection just as important? Why don't we celebrate those?"

"We do," I said. "On Good Friday and Easter."

"Oh, is that what that's all about?" he said. This young man had grown up in the United States yet he didn't know the meaning of Easter!

Scripture and Ritual Practices

Meditating on Scripture is an important source of nourishment for any Christian, but especially for the traditionalist. And this repetitive practice was first recommended back in Old Testament times: "Do not let this Book of the Law depart from your mouth; meditate on it day and night, so that you may be careful to do everything written in it."[13]

Certain scriptural rituals can actually add new meaning to an old practice. Consider trying the following:

Read Scripture aloud. I began doing this in a hotel room once. I was on the road and tired; when I tried to silently read the Bible, the words seemed to melt into one another and I was getting nowhere. I knew I needed to be replenished, however, so I got up, paced around the room, and began reading the Scriptures aloud. At that point the words came alive. Hearing them spoken seemed to ram them into my soul.

Use the Psalms. The great, early church father Chrysostom took it for granted that every Christian read through Psalm 62 in the morning and Psalm 140 in the evening. According to Caesarious of

Arles, all Christians knew Psalms 50, 90, and 103.[14] There can be great benefit in reading the same passages of Scripture over and over until you know them by heart. Imagine the power of reading a psalm at age eighty that you read daily in your thirties. Rituals can tie our years together with the common thread of faith.

Begin your day with the Bible. In my early teens I started the practice of reading a chapter of the Bible first thing in the morning and last thing in the evening—my first and last conscious activity would be God's Word. I've heard of another Christian who places his Bible on his shoes at night. Before he can get dressed the next morning, he'll need to read the Scriptures.

The Christian Calendar

Christianity is based on God breaking into the physical world, most noticeably in the incarnation or the birth of Christ.[15] This is why celebrating the Christian calendar can be such a help to Christian worship.

When we ritualize historic events, not just Christmas and Easter but Pentecost and Advent and Ascension Day as well, we affirm that our spiritual worship is historically based.

I also like to add more contemporary reminders to my calendar as well, perhaps a reminder of Pascal's ecstatic experience on November 23, 1664, or Bonhoeffer's imprisonment and eventual martyrdom on April 9, 1945, or Augustine's birth—any events that may have particular meaning because a historic figure has influenced my faith.

On these days, you can read a portion of the particular Christian's work or just ponder the contribution his or her life made to the history of Christianity. This time of remembrance inspires us to do our part, however limited, to also build up the body of Christ.

A Rule of Prayer

To bring structure to prayer, many Christians have found it helpful to establish a "rule" or "habit" of prayer, which helps them to pray every day.

Since the intention is to repeat this practice every day, it's best to keep this liturgical time relatively short. You can always add to it, but you might be more tempted to skip it if the basic rule is too long.

I've found repetitive prayers to be helpful, not because that makes it more likely that God hears my prayers, but because it helps me understand more fully what I am praying.

To develop your own rule, you might survey some Episcopalian or Eastern Orthodox prayer books. When using the latter, evangelical Christians will want to delete the hymns or prayers to Mary, but much that remains can be very helpful.

The following is a sample rule compiled by Marc Dunaway. I've taken the liberty of making some omissions and a few additions; the full outline with some additional suggested prayers is available in the booklet from which this was taken, *Building a Habit of Prayer,* published by Conciliar Press in 1989.

Invocation

In the name of the Father and the Son and the Holy Spirit. Amen.

(Short time of silence)

O God, be merciful to me, a sinner. (repeat three times)

[Note: I've found repetitive prayers to be helpful, not because that makes it more likely that God hears my prayers, but because it helps me understand more fully what I am praying.]

Prayer of Cleansing
Psalm 51

Lord, cleanse me of my sins and have mercy on me.

Prayer to the Holy Spirit

Glory to You, O Lord. Glory to You.
O Heavenly King, O Comforter, the Spirit of truth, the Treasure of good things and Giver of life, come and abide in us. Cleanse us from every stain and save our souls, O Good One.

The Trisagion Prayers

Holy God, Holy Mighty, Holy Immortal, have mercy on us. (repeat three times)

Glory to the Father and to the Son and to the Holy Spirit, now and forever. Amen.

O Most Holy Trinity, have mercy on us.

O Lord, cleanse us from our sins.

O Master, pardon our iniquities.

O Holy One, visit and heal our infirmities for Your Name's sake.

Lord, have mercy. (repeat three times)

Glory to the Father and to the Son and to the Holy Spirit, now and forever. Amen.

Our Father, Who art in heaven, hallowed be Thy Name. Thy kingdom come, Thy will be done on earth as it is in heaven. Give us this day our daily bread, and forgive us our trespasses as we forgive those who trespass against us. And lead us not into temptation, but deliver us from evil. For Thine is the kingdom and the power and the glory for ever and ever. Amen.

Lord, have mercy. (repeat three times)

Call to Worship

Come, let us worship and bow down before God our King.

Come, let us worship and bow down before Christ, our King and our God.

Come, let us worship and bow down before Christ Himself, our King and our God.

Song (optional)

"Come Let Us Worship and Bow Down" (or something similar)

Read or sing a psalm

Read Scripture

Follow through on your own schedule

Choose a hymn or song for the day

Intercessions

Bring your own spontaneous personal requests before God, or follow an intercessory list that you have developed on your own. You may want to include some time for God to lay some requests (or words of instruction) on your heart.

Closing Prayer

Glory to the Father and to the Son and to the Holy Spirit, now and forever. Amen.

Lord, have mercy. (three times)

O Lord, thank You for hearing my prayers. Give me the strength to serve You this day. Have mercy on me and save me, for You are good and love humankind. Amen.

Some people may find that such structure hinders their prayers; but others, particularly those who struggle with wandering thoughts or who are new to praying, may find that this form will help their prayers improve in both their discipline and sincerity.

New Christians often need more guidance than the popular "Just talk to God, tell him what's on your heart" to learn how to pray properly.

The evangelical movement has suffered somewhat from making prayers too informal. New Christians often need more guidance than the popular "Just talk to God, tell him what's on your heart" to learn how to pray properly. Praying according to a rule can school a Christian to pray appropriately—with adoration, thanksgiving, and confession tied together with intercession.

An alternative rule of prayer that I've also found to be helpful is to pray through the Lord's Prayer, pausing with each line to personalize it. In this way, I use the Lord's Prayer as the basic structure for my own spontaneous prayers. It's a good mix.

Scheduled Prayer

Throughout Christian history, believers have often held that prayer is far too important to be left to chance. On the contrary, early

Christians saw disciplined times set aside for prayer as the only way to be faithful in prayer.

Clement of Alexandria, a major Christian writer in the late second century, tells us that many Christians fixed hours to be assigned for prayer, such as the third, the sixth, and the ninth. Canticles of praise and Scripture readings were usually undertaken before meals and sleep.[16]

The Didache, an early Christian document, states that first-century Christians were expected to pray three times each day, usually using the Lord's Prayer. Tertullian, a Christian leader in the early third century, urged prayer during the third, sixth, and ninth hours, like Clement of Alexandria. This was in addition to regular prayers that were offered at the beginning of the day and during the night.

Rituals provide structure for our faith. Once we learn to use them, traditionalists can also incorporate the use of symbols, which provide meaning.

Tertullian also stressed, however, that hours were guides more than rules. Christians need to pray at least three times daily, he said, and set times can help accomplish this aim.[17]

When I first began spending daily time in prayer, I often grew frustrated at how I could forget about God's presence by lunchtime, even after praying for an hour in the morning. Shorter but more frequent times of prayer may actually help us to live with an increasing awareness of God's presence in our lives. How difficult would it be for us to set aside five minutes in the morning, five minutes at noon, and five minutes before or after dinnertime to meet God in prayer?

Rituals provide structure for our faith. Once we learn to use them, traditionalists can also incorporate the use of symbols, which provide meaning.

Symbols

How many times have you heard a moving sermon, been almost knocked over by a powerful verse, or been given a great new insight, only to lose its effect because you forgot about it so soon after it was given? Symbols can help us overcome one of the great difficulties of the Christian life—the problem of a poor memory.

Dietrich Bonhoeffer, the German Christian who was martyred for standing against Hitler, was fascinated by how his fellow prisoners could come so close to death in an air raid and then forget about it as soon as the danger was past. While allied bombs rocked the prison cells, nonbelieving men would cry out to God for salvation; but as soon as the bombers had passed and the dust settled, the prisoners went back to playing cards and passing time, forgetting all about their supplications to God. Bonhoeffer writes:

> Something that repeatedly puzzles me as well as other people is how quickly we forget about our impressions of a night's bombing. Even a few minutes after the all clear, almost everything that we had just been thinking about seems to vanish into thin air. With Luther a flash of lightning was enough to change the course of his life for years to come. Where is this "memory" today? Is not the loss of this "moral memory" responsible for the ruin of all obligations, of love, marriage, friendship, and loyalty? Nothing sticks fast, nothing holds firm; everything is here today and gone tomorrow.

> But the good things of life—truth, justice, and beauty—all great accomplishments need time, constancy, and "memory," or they degenerate. The man who feels neither responsibility towards the past nor desire to shape the future is one who "forgets," and I don't know how one can really get at such a person and bring him to his senses. Every word, even if it impresses him for the moment, goes in at one ear and out at the other. What is to be done about him? It is a great problem of Christian ministry.[18]

Symbols help us to preserve this "moral memory," which is so essential to right living.

God endorsed the use of symbols when he spoke to Moses, saying, "Speak to the Israelites and say to them: 'Throughout the generations to come you are to make tassels on the corners of your garments, with a blue cord on each tassel. You will have these tassels to look at and so you will remember all the commands of the LORD, that you may obey them and not prostitute yourselves by going after the lusts of your own hearts and eyes. Then you will remember to obey all my commands and will be consecrated to your God.'"[19]

I can hear the cries of resistance: "But we're saved by faith! We don't need those Old Testament symbols!" Symbols have nothing to do with saving us, but they have everything to do with realizing the effects of that salvation upon our everyday lives. Just because we're saved doesn't mean we don't need help to live holy lives.

A Christian who has a hard time living by his or her faith while driving, for instance, could hang a symbol—a cross or a fish—on their rearview mirror to challenge them when their temper begins to flare. (That's certainly preferable to putting a Christian bumper sticker on the back of the car for all to see, and then driving like a son of perdition!) A pastor friend of mine uses a pond near his home as a symbol. As soon as he drives by that pond, he is reminded that he is going home and needs to prepare himself to focus on his wife and children, leaving the cares, worries, and concerns of the church on the north side of the pond. He can pick them back up the next morning when he passes the pond on his way to work.

A symbol can be found to meet virtually every need in every situation. Men or women who have failed sexually can begin wearing a cross as a reminder of their pledge to now remain pure. Others might choose to wear a ring during certain periods of intensive prayer; every time they see the ring they will be reminded of their prayer.

> Symbols have nothing to do with saving us, but they have everything to do with realizing the effects of that salvation upon our everyday lives. Just because we're saved doesn't mean we don't need help to live holy lives.

One of the symbols that Bonhoeffer found helpful in prison was making the sign of the cross during prayer. To one who is familiar with Bonhoeffer's writings, this is incredibly significant. At that point in his life, Bonhoeffer was seeking a "religionless" Christianity, but his experiment failed. Bonhoeffer found, as many Christians have, that symbols can be potent ushers of God's presence and reality.

Architects use Christian symbols. Byzantine churches, for example, often resemble the shape of a cross. Other churches were constructed in circular form, symbolizing that "the church has been extended throughout the circle of the world." Still other churches use elements of the building for symbolic purposes. The nave of a church, where the congregation sits, takes its name from the Latin word *navis,* or ship, symbolizing the ship of the church tossed on the waves of the world, similar also to the picture of Noah's ark. The chancel, where the choir sits, is symbolic of the church triumphant.[20]

> *The "alb" . . . is unusually beautiful symbolism— to be buried in clothes proclaiming the hope of baptism.*

Some Christian traditions have made symbols out of baptism cloths, called the "alb," which are kept as a memorial of the baptism and used as a covering for the body after death. This, I think, is unusually beautiful symbolism—to be buried in clothes proclaiming the hope of baptism.

Evangelicals, of course, use bread and wine or juice as symbols of Christ's body and blood. The Christian church historically has also made great use of symbols for the members of the Trinity. Christ is frequently symbolized by the chi-rho symbol, which looks like the letter P over the letter X. These are the first two Greek letters in *Christ.* I.H.S. is also used, the first three Greek letters in the word *Jesus.* The five letters inside the fish are the first letters of the Greek spelling of Jesus Christ, God, Son, Savior. Jesus' deity and lordship were symbolized by a picture of a shepherd—the Good Shepherd. His passion and suffering were captured in a picture of the Lamb.[21]

God the Father was generally not symbolized in early Christianity. He was only to be revealed through the incarnate Christ, so there were never any earthly pictures to copy. However, up until perhaps the twelfth century, God the Father was sometimes represented by a hand. In the thirteenth and fourteenth centuries, an arm was added, signifying the arm of the Lord. Later, God the Father was pictured as an aged man, and still later, in the West, as the pope with multiple crowns (the earthly pope had just one crown).[22]

I am not advocating that we return to these symbols. Personally, I agree with early Christian theologians who rejected depictions of God the Father. Something as nebulous as a hand may legitimately serve art, but pictures of an aged man don't do justice to God the Father. It is one thing to depict Jesus, who was incarnate; it is dangerous to depict the Father, whom we have not seen.

The Holy Spirit, of course, is frequently symbolized as a dove (reminiscent of the Bible's metaphor of the Holy Spirit settling on Jesus) or with fire (reminiscent of the day of Pentecost when "tongues of fire" rested on the heads of the disciples). The Trinity historically has been symbolized by a triangle or three entwined circles.[23]

Christian art made use of many different symbols that modern traditionalist temperaments may find helpful in their homes, offices, and cars. Some of these symbols include an anchor (hope, the last hope of sailors); an arrow (martyrdom, pain, suffering); a banner (triumph over persecution and death); a circle (eternity); a crown (sovereignty); a lamp (wisdom and piety); a palm (martyrdom); and the square (earthly existence).[24]

The cross has frequently been one of the major symbols of Christianity, but even this symbol has many variations. Anyone who has looked at an Eastern Orthodox catalog knows an Orthodox cross looks different from one that might be worn by a Protestant. And the Protestant's cross certainly looks much different from a Roman Catholic crucifix. The symbol of the cross has changed through the centuries. In the early Middle Ages, Christ was usually depicted on the cross, signifying the suffering Savior. In earlier antiquity, however, the cross was usually depicted without the figure of the crucified, signifying the *empty* cross as a symbol of Christian victory.

Early Christian artists used colors for symbolism, as do current liturgical churches. Though this symbolism varied somewhat, in general, white was used on Easter and Christmas and as a color of joy. Red spoke of the exaltation of the cross, feasts of the martyrs, and the Lord's passion. Green symbolized common Sundays and ordinary weekdays, as well as being the symbol of life (plants and vegetables). Purple was used for Lent, Holy Week, and Advent, and spoke of the union of love and pain. Black was used only on Good Friday.[25]

A more sophisticated form of symbolism involves the use of gargoyles, which are used to exalt the pure, noble, beautiful, and good, by contrasting them with the ugly, coarse, and vulgar. Some people, however, have polluted these symbols with superstition. Superstition is to religion what lust is to love, an empty substitute that misses the power of the original.

Symbols also become dangerous if they become the center (rather than a reminder) of our faith. This happened in Old Testament history. On one such occasion, God commanded Moses to build a bronze snake so that Israel could be healed from a plague of snakebites. Later in history, Israel began worshiping the snake, treating it as a god rather than a symbol.[26] Something good can be perverted, but the perversion is in the use of the symbol, not the symbol itself.

> *Superstition is to religion what lust is to love, an empty substitute that misses the power of the original.*

Gertrud Mueller Nelson, a contemporary writer, writes a beautiful passage about rituals and symbols bringing a needed "poetry" into our worship:

> What we have lost touch with lies in the poetic aspect of the Church which has ... nourished us through rite and symbol, through rhythmic repetition.... This creative and poetic Church helps us to pay full attention to what we might otherwise deem ordinary and commonplace. Rites and symbols use the ordinary and earthy elements of our existence and, by encircling them, ratify, sanctify, complete. The ordinary becomes the container for the divine and safely holds what was uncontainable. The transcendent is disclosed in what is wonderfully familiar: bread, wine, fire, ash, earth, water, oil, tears, seeds, songs, feasting and fasting, pains and joys.... It draws its action more from what is most human in us than from theology. In its creative function, the Church speaks directly to the heart, a heart which hears symbols, not rational vocabulary.[27]

Sacrifice

The third element of traditionalists' faith—besides ritual and the use of symbols—is sacrifice. Sacrifice is at the heart of Christianity. Those who want to identify with their Lord, who gave the supreme sacrifice, must understand this. Sacrifice keeps our idealized and often romantic expressions of divine adoration rooted in reality. Worship must not be reduced to mere emotional expression, for Christianity calls us to a commitment of the will.

The notion of sacrifice is also at the heart of why so many traditionalists celebrate Lent. Unfortunately, we are a culture that celebrates Mardi Gras but rarely gets around to Lent! "Liberated" Christians may well ask, "Why observe Lent?" God doesn't need us to give up anything; certainly, he doesn't "need" my meat, but sometimes I need to learn to deny myself something in order to truly appreciate what really matters.

One year, I decided to give up ice cream for Lent. Since I was raised as a Baptist, I had never even considered observing this season, but our family decided to give it a try. During this period, I was traveling and stopped at a grocery store to get something to eat. Unfortunately, it was an out-of-the-way grocery store and the produce looked like it had been trucked in from Brazil—three weeks prior. There was no real bread, to speak of, and nothing that looked appetizing enough to take back to my hotel room.

Finally, I gave in to the "dark side." "I'll just get a small carton of ice cream," I thought. But as soon as my hand hit that cold container I remembered my commitment—and put the ice cream back. Suddenly, I was vividly reminded of the Easter season; what Christ had done on our behalf broke into my consciousness and my Easter "mourning and celebrating" was deepened.

All in all, I'd say it was a fabulously good trade forgoing the ice cream to live with a deeper sense of the Easter season. That's what fasting is all about, isn't it? This doesn't earn us any extra merit or favors with God, but God can use it to chasten our demanding hearts.

Of course, we can't really give anything to God—everything is his, including the strength by which we sacrifice—but the notion of performing a sacrifice reminds us that we are God's servants and that God is not our servant.

There are three types of sacrifice in the Old Testament: the sin offering, the guilt offering, and the burnt offering. (All sacrifices are offerings, but not all offerings are sacrifices.)[28] Some offerings allowed the giver to use the item offered (a singer might sacrifice her voice to the Lord) while others were totally consumed (an alcoholic might decide to never taste alcohol again). Our sacrifices might include giving up something permanently or dedicating something to the Lord's use. The giving of our money should be seen as a sacrifice, something we are giving to God that can't be used by us for another purpose.

Sacrifice is at the heart of a holy life. At times we will be called to give up something we cherish that has illicitly nourished us in the past—an inappropriate relationship, a job that provides financial security, an activity, overeating, gambling, smoking.

The prophetic denunciations of sacrifice that scare many Christians away from talking about this as a way to love God are directed at the degradation of the ritual, not the idea of it.[29] God endorses the concept of sacrifice throughout the Old Testament, and Jesus participated in the sacrificial system in the New Testament, ultimately becoming a sacrifice himself. Of course, Christ's sacrifice made animal sacrifice obsolete, but the principle still remained operative: Paul exhorted the Romans to offer themselves as a living sacrifice.[30] Admittedly, in context, Paul is urging us to offer our spiritual gifts to serve the body of Christ: merely "giving up" something could actually trivialize Paul's admonition rather than fulfill it. The point, however, is to understand the nature of sacrifice in the Christian life, and how sacrifice is part of what a healthy Christian does.

> *"Faith" today is often seen as a tool to get something special from God. Historically a man or woman of faith is one who was willing to give something precious to God.*

Traditionalists remind us that we have turned our faith inside out. "Faith" today is often seen as a tool to get something special *from* God. Historically a man or woman of faith is one who was willing to give something precious *to* God. When the traditionalist incorporates the idea of sacrifice into his or her daily life, a key component of Christianity is modeled and preserved.

Living as a Traditionalist

How, then, can you love God as a traditionalist? By incorporating the three elements of this temperament into your daily life: Make plentiful use of symbols; develop meaningful rituals; and find areas of sacrifice.

I would encourage you to begin by adopting one of the categories—symbols, for instance—and then slowly bring their use into your life. You might even want to read further about ancient Christian symbols to give you more background. As symbols are incorporated into your worship, consider adding another category. Perhaps you could add one ritual a year, a certain way to begin Christmas morning, a special Sunday prayer, a new form of Bible reading, and so on.

The glory of life in Christ is that we are starting a life that will go on for eternity. We certainly don't need to rush! Meaning is more important than accomplishment; symbolism must be the servant, not the master, of substance. Go slowly, and gradually bring the religious element into your life.

The Temptations of Traditionalists
Serving God Without Knowing God

It is possible to serve God religiously for quite some time without actually knowing him. Samuel is a good example of this danger. First Samuel 3:1 tells us that "the boy Samuel ministered before the LORD under Eli," yet in verse seven we're told, "Samuel did not yet know the LORD: The word of the LORD had not yet been revealed to him." Samuel was intimately involved in the religious observances of Israel, but he didn't know the God of Israel personally.

The world is full of religions and religious people who don't know God. Religion can serve faith, but it doesn't substitute for faith, and it can never replace faith. Meaningful expressions of the heart, mind, and will become lifeless if they're not mixed with a deep and abiding faith.

Neglecting Social Obligations

Like several other spiritual temperaments, traditionalists may get so caught up in their faith, they forget the social obligations of faith. It is not enough for us to cultivate holiness; we must reach out and minister to others.

Remember God's warning to the Israelites: "I hate, I despise your religious feasts; I cannot stand your assemblies. Even though you bring me burnt offerings and grain offerings, I will not accept them. Though you bring choice fellowship offerings, I will have no regard for them. Away with the noise of your songs! I will not listen to the music of your harps. But let justice roll on like a river, righteousness like a never-failing stream!"[31]

Substituting religion for the social obligations of the faith must have been a constant temptation for Israel, for Jeremiah also warns that religion alone is not enough. "Do not trust in deceptive words and say, 'This is the temple of the LORD, the temple of the LORD, the temple of the LORD!' If you really change your ways and your actions and deal with each other justly, if you do not oppress the alien, the fatherless or the widow and do not shed innocent blood in this place, and if you do not follow other gods to your own harm, then I will let you live in this place."[32]

Jesus also warned against empty displays of religion. Religion without substance, says Christ, is hypocrisy; it makes us "white-washed tombs, which look beautiful on the outside but on the inside are full of dead men's bones and everything unclean."[33]

Judging Others

Traditionalists must remember that God, not religion, is sacred. It took a vivid noontime vision for Peter to relinquish the religious food prohibitions that blocked him from reaching out to the Gentiles.[34] Paul's life calling to minister to the Gentiles made him particularly careful not to elevate religious rituals to the measurement of true faith. He makes it clear in Romans 14 and Colossians 2:16–17 that religious observances are to be used for self-edification, not for judging others: "Do not let anyone judge you by what you eat or drink, or with regard to a religious festival, a New Moon celebration or a Sabbath day. These are a shadow of the things that were to come; the reality, however, is found in Christ."[35] Paul warns Timothy against those who, in the name of religion, forbid Christians to participate in activities which God created for their enjoyment and pleasure.[36]

Traditionalists should freely engage in those rituals and observances that build up their faith, but just because something is beneficial to them doesn't mean it is obligatory to others.

> *Religious observances are to be used for self-edification, not for judging others.*

Near the hometown where I grew up, a conservative Baptist pastor "shocked" some of his parishioners because he enjoyed gardening on Sunday afternoon. This pastor spent his entire week studying Scripture, and he found that gardening was not work as much as it was relaxation as he prepared for the evening service even though that didn't square with some parishioners' view of the Sabbath.

Religion can powerfully enhance an individual's faith, but it can also destroy corporate faith if it is used to criticize, measure, or divide.

Repeating Mechanically

Imbued with a vibrant faith, the repetition of ritual is a powerful force for good. Without present attention, however, ritual becomes an empty exercise that floods our souls with insincerity. Rituals, especially personal ones, can be changed. If something has lost its life for you, adopt something else. (I am speaking about personal rather than corporate worship, of course.)

Deifying Rites

The new pastor thought his benediction closed the service so he poured his heart into it, but when he opened his eyes he saw his church members joining hands and the pianist walking up to her piano. One of the deacons gestured to the new pastor to step down, and as the pastor did so, the congregation began singing, "Blessed be the tie that binds." The church had sung the song after every Communion as long as anyone could remember. With or without the new pastor's cooperation, the song was going to stay.

In this instance, such a circumstance can be a humorous anecdote for seminary classes rather than representing any real harm; in other circumstances, such attitudes can be lethal. People have a tendency to virtually deify something just because that's the way it's always been done, even if they no longer understand why it is done.

No symbol and no ritual has absolute value in itself.[37] A symbol represents a hidden reality; it is there to evoke the mysterious. When the original meaning is lost, the symbol is of no more value than an expired coupon.

Are You a Traditionalist?

Are you a traditionalist? Score the series of statements below on a scale of five to one, with five being very true and one being not true at all. Record your answer in the space provided.

_____ 1. I feel closest to God when I'm participating in a familiar form of worship that has memories dating back to my childhood. Rituals and traditions move me more than anything else.

_____ 2. Individualism within the church is a real danger. Christianity is a corporate faith, and most of our worship should have a corporate expression.

_____ 3. The words tradition and history are very appealing to me.

_____ 4. Participating in a formal liturgy or prayer-book service, developing symbols that I could place in my car, home, or office, and developing a Christian calendar for our family to follow are activities that I would enjoy.

_____ 5. A book titled Symbolism and Liturgy in Personal Worship would be appealing to me.

_____ 6. I would really enjoy developing a personal rule (or ritual) of prayer.

The total of all your answers. _____

Again any score of fifteen or higher indicates a preference for this spiritual temperament. Take a moment to register this score in chapter eleven on page 217 to develop your composite picture.

Discovering Traditionalism

During college, I cut my teeth on "spontaneous" Christianity, almost to a fault. The more "holy" you were, I thought, the more willing you would be to "move with the Spirit." People who wrote out prayers (and at one point, I thought, even sermons) beforehand were coming dangerously close to "quenching the Spirit."

Thus when I first encountered liturgy, set prayers, and various religious practices, I was surprised by how deeply my soul responded. I'm tempted to describe it as "coming home," except I was never there in the first place!

Still, I felt I had touched my roots.

And I had.

Many of the religious obligations I had felt "delivered" from in my own youth, I later discovered as potential avenues of spiritual growth. Instead of feeling delivered, I felt cheated, as if I had been taught to live the Christian life without being given something very helpful to assist me.

The Christian faith is a faith based in history and community. Ritual, symbols, sacraments, and sacrifice have marked its entire history. Virtually every symbol, ritual, or rite has probably gotten in the way at one time or another, or veered off course, however slightly, or fallen into rote repetition, losing its power.

But the real problem, I found, was not with the symbol, ritual, or rite, but with the human heart. Many of the religious obligations I had felt "delivered" from in my own youth, I later discovered as potential avenues of spiritual growth. Instead of feeling delivered, I felt cheated, as if I had been taught to live the Christian life without being given something very helpful to assist me. I feel carried by their power, nurtured by their truth, and strengthened by their practice.

Maybe you will, too.

FIVE

ASCETICS: LOVING GOD IN SOLITUDE AND SIMPLICITY

Dressed in an animal skin, John the Baptist pranced around the amphitheater, screaming out his defiance of the Pharisees. His hair was knotted and his muscles were taut with tension. He picked up a fistful of dirt and cast it into the air, and the dirt showered him as he screamed, the veins on his neck bulging like fire hoses bursting with pressure. He was berating Herod, and demanding that he repent.

John's voice had two volumes—loud and louder. His heavy, labored breathing had an asthmatic quality to it as he paced back and forth like a caged animal, spittle flying out of his mouth as he spewed his denouncements.

Was this an accurate portrayal of John the Baptist? I doubt it. For starters, he couldn't have preached more than thirty minutes at that pace and volume, much less for hours a day, day after day. Furthermore, just because John the Baptist had taken what appeared to be a vow of the Nazirite, abstaining from alcohol, avoiding dead bodies, not cutting his hair, and so forth, doesn't mean he had chosen to live on the precipice of insanity.

That John the Baptist was so portrayed in this passion play doesn't surprise me, though. Our culture has a difficult time understanding the ascetic temperament. We might admire these people, but we often suspect them of religious fanaticism, which we see as a cousin to mental illness.

The ascetic temperament gravitates toward solitude, austerity, simplicity, and deep commitment. It's the "monastic" temperament, so to speak, representing believers who aren't afraid of discipline, severity, and solitude—indeed, believers who find that these elements awaken their souls to God's presence.

It's ironic that in a culture where loneliness and isolation are almost pandemic, solitude is so foreign to us. One reason for this is that we have lost the art of austerity, which gives meaning and substance to our solitude. The word *austere* has a number of connotations: it can mean morally strict, somber or grave, unadorned or simple. All of these meanings are relevant here, and they point out why the ascetic is such an enigmatic figure to us.

> *Most of our solitude is forced, not chosen, creating loneliness rather than spiritual intimacy with the Father.*

Most of our solitude is forced, not chosen, creating loneliness rather than spiritual intimacy with the Father, and our culture is anything but morally strict. We gravitate toward the trite and trivial rather than the somber and grave, and we pride ourselves on adornment and complexity rather than simplicity, often because many of us are trying desperately to hide our true selves. Ascetics, perhaps more than any of the other spiritual temperaments, must truly go against their culture to practice loving God.

The Bible and Ascetics

Growing up, I was always fascinated by the Nazirite. *That's what it means to be holy,* I thought. *Give up everything you have, and look really weird.*

Of course, I was wrong. Nazirites were not so much people as vows taken for a set period of time during which the adherents agreed to abstain from alcohol, refrain from cutting their hair (I liked that part, but my dad never bought it!), and stay away from contact with a dead body. During the period of this vow, Nazirites were in essence pictures of holiness—literally "set apart" for a special purpose. Because the Nazirites' vows were only for a set period of time, they could leave their solitude to later fulfill the social obligations of their faith.[1]

John the Baptist immediately comes to mind when we think of the solitary and the ascetic, but Jesus also had these tendencies. Before he launched himself into his public ministry, Jesus spent forty days in solitude and fasting. He taught that prayer should be done in secret; he assumed that his disciples would eventually fast. And he returned to solitude at difficult moments in his ministry—after hearing about John the Baptist's death and when the crowds pursued him, for instance.[2]

Mark, as well as Matthew, also tells us that Christ frequently sought solitude. "Very early in the morning, while it was still dark, Jesus got up, left the house and went off to a solitary place, where he prayed."[3] Mark's choice of words, here translated "solitary place," could also mean "deserted," connoting the barrenness of the surroundings. Even a lush place seems austere in the dark, however. It's not surprising then, that before his greatest test, Jesus found comfort in the dark, in the Garden of Gethsemane, kneeling quietly and privately in prayer.[4]

It is in these dark, intense, and lonely times that ascetics' souls awaken. I think that anyone who has been stretched in ministry knows that the real battle was fought at Gethsemane, not Calvary. To be sure, only Calvary provided payment for our sins and thus was absolutely necessary, but Gethsemane was the real spiritual battleground where Jesus made the final decision to be obedient. In a wrenching, courageous act of self-denial, Jesus proved the mettle of his faith.

When I was involved in street preaching on college campuses, the soul-wrenching and gut-busting struggles came during the moments in prayer before I actually spoke. Once I had wrestled with my fears and my doubts, the act of obedience became almost anticlimactic. Even later in life, as I've struggled with God's will, the act of obedience always seems less difficult than the prior decision to be obedient. "Don't you know where God is leading on this?" I was asked once.

"Yes, I do," I said. "And that's the problem. I'm waiting for my willingness to catch up with God's."

That's why I identify so much with Christ, alone and in agony, as he prayed in Gethsemane. It is the ultimate picture of Christianity, the picture of us struggling spiritually as God aligns our will with his. It's the picture that fuels the ascetic spiritual temperament.

The Old Testament gives us several profiles of ascetics, not just in the Nazirite, but in a call for the devout to mourn. The Psalms provide treasured passages for enthusiasts who love to celebrate, but Lamentations, Daniel, and Joel provide many rich passages for ascetics who know they are called to mourn.

Daniel writes of fervent prayer in which he pleads with God, fasts, and sits in sackcloth and ashes.[5] Joel urges the spiritual leaders to wear sackcloth, to mourn, wail, fast, and spend the night watching in prayer, crying out to God. God himself urges Israel to return to him with fasting, weeping, and mourning.[6]

Certainly, then, there is a time and place for the role of austerity and solitude in every Christian's worship. For those with this particular spiritual temperament, however, these two qualities may be the most cherished forms of worship.

The Three Worlds of Ascetics

To give a more precise definition of this temperament, we can break it down into three worlds: solitude, austerity, and strictness.

Solitude

Over the years, solitude has become one of my best friends. There is a quiet and depth to solitude that nourishes me while other spiritual activities—preaching, for instance—deplete me. Even in a crowd or party, sometimes I'll try to "sneak in" a few moments of solitude. Some might argue that in doing this I'm taking myself too seriously, and they may be right. All I know is that it's in those solitary moments that colors regain their brightness, truth regains its clarity, and reality loses its fog. Without some time alone, I feel like I've lost my anchor.

M. Basil Pennington said, "If one note is to characterize the true monk, it is this: He is the one who has gone apart, to be in some way alone."[7] Modern-day "monks" recognize that even if they are married or in a busy church ministry, spending some time apart is essential for a deepening walk with God.

For a young mother or father, or a child living at home, getting completely away may not be possible; the important thing, however, is "the sense of apartness."[8] A family might create a prayer room; perhaps your local church will allow you to have keys to the sanctuary. Just the act of getting away can serve as a call or prelude to worship.

Solitude is essential in that ascetics live fundamentally internal existences. Jerome, a fouth-century ascetic, wrote that "to me the town is a prison, and solitude is paradise."[9] While I'm very sympathetic to Jerome's confession, I've also learned that there is a temptation in this. Solitude is a tool when we use it to recharge; if we neglect "the town," however, we won't be able to reach those who most need our message.

> *Solitude has become one of my best friends.*

Informed ascetics will rightly respond that an individual's prayers are rivers running into the ocean of the church. Evelyn Underhill, a popular British writer and speaker on the spiritual life in the early part of this century, wrote, "Each Christian life of prayer . . . however deeply hidden or apparently solitary in form, will affect the life of the whole Body. By the very fact of its entrance into the sphere of worship, its action is added to that total sacrifice of praise and thanksgiving in which the life of the church invisible consists."[10]

Historically, the emphasis on solitary living, which marked early asceticism, gradually gave way to learning to live in detachment within society. Solitude evolved into duos consisting of a master and disciple, then small groups, and then larger communities. "Dying to others, one of the basic requirements of a solitary ascetic, became more an inner disposition, quite compatible with proximity to other men."[11] Jerome particularly stressed "inner asceticism." According to him, virginity, leaving the city, and poverty were beginning points, not the end, of asceticism.[12] A later ascetic took this inner detachment a step further, saying, "Let her find in the busy city the desert of the monks."[13]

This is the lifeline for modern ascetics. We don't have to find a desert to express our faith; inner detachment allows us to find a lonely desert in the midst of the busiest city. For years I thrived on arriving hours before anyone else came to the office because the quiet and solitude were essential for my faith. The early morning was my favorite part of the day. When another "early bird" was hired, it took some time for me to adjust. Friends and families will need to learn that ascetics need a certain amount of time alone, perhaps every day.

Austerity

A friend of our family, a young woman with two small children, exhibits many ascetic traits. Her closest moments with God occur when the kids have gone to bed, all the lights are turned out, and everything is quiet. If the kids won't be quiet, she's been known to go into the bathroom, turn on the faucet to block other noise, and pray to God there.

While sensate Christians are drawn to God through their senses, ascetic Christians are often distracted by their senses so they will try to shut them out.

Susanna Wesley, mother of John and Charles Wesley, raised a large family but, like the mother just mentioned, craved an austere and solitary place from which she could meet her God. Her solution? She frequently pulled her apron over her head and prayed. Her kids learned not to bother her during that time. While sensate Christians are drawn to God through their senses, ascetic Christians are often distracted by their senses so they will try to shut them out. Monks often chose environments with low levels of sensory input so that they wouldn't be distracted in their prayer and fasting.[14] While Francis of Assisi reveled in the beauty of the countryside, many of the desert fathers sought out barren wastelands. It is here where the ascetic may part company with the naturalist.

Strictness

A decade ago, with some dismay, I found that what they often say about ten-year high school reunions is true: Women do tend to look prettier, men do tend to gain weight and lose hair, and people are still trying to make impressions. I wasn't expecting, however, one of the little rumors that had been floating around.

"Did you hear about Gary?" one rumor went. "He sold everything he owned, joined a religious group, and became a religious fanatic."

"Is that true?" one person asked me.

I laughed. "It only feels like it. The truth is, I went to seminary, moved into a house that cost $200 a month to rent, and worked for a campus ministry that paid me about what you would expect a campus ministry to pay you."

My wife was rather alarmed when she heard what had been said, but I was more amused. Ninety-nine percent of communication is in the interpretation. A man who begins giving a portion of his income to the church and its work, carves out time two or three times a week to attend church services, tells people on the street about his God, and reads books about God on a regular basis may appear to the world to be a "religious fanatic." If, however, the same man were to begin making payments on a diamond ring, spend his weekends going on dates, tell all his coworkers about the lovely woman who has come into his life, and read love letters over and over, the world would simply say he's "in love."

If I were to write an entire book on asceticism, I would be tempted to entitle it *The Divine Romance*. We normally don't think of asceticism and strictness as allies of romance, but they are. Ascetics are "strict" only because they want to reserve a major portion of their lives for their passionate pursuit of God.

It is this strict side of the ascetic's life that is perhaps the least understood, not only by our culture, but also by other Christians. Especially among evangelicals, who champion salvation by grace through faith, a strict faith can seem perilously close to legalism; and in some cases, it might be. For healthy ascetics, however, strictness is a cherished method of expressing love for God.

In a book on the life of Francis of Assisi, G. K. Chesterton answers those who ask, "What cruel kind of God can have demanded sacrifice and self-denial?" by putting the question in another context. What selfish sort of woman, he asks, would demand flowers or be so avaricious as to demand a gold ring to wear on her finger? "It was because the thing was not demanded that it was done," Chesterton writes, and in doing so he reminds us of the romantic side to asceticism.[15]

Chesterton says that the popular view of the ascetic, that of the gloomy, depressed person, is in error. "The whole point about St. Francis of Assisi is that he certainly was ascetical and he certainly was not gloomy. He devoured fasting as a man devours food. He plunged after poverty as men have dug madly for gold. And it is precisely the positive and passionate quality of this part of his personality that is a challenge to the modern mind in the whole problem of the pursuit of pleasure."[16]

True Christian asceticism doesn't seek suffering or self-denial as an end, but as a means, as a way to love "something else that God might be loved more."[17]

Thus the ascetic life has historically been intimately tied with mystical theology, also known as the contemplative life. I am drawing a distinction between the two as I discuss spiritual temperaments. In the modern, popular world, I think they've split apart, but historically, one went hand in hand with the other. Ascetics lived strict lives of self-denial so that they would be free to contemplate God. Without self-denial, sins of the flesh arose and made it impossible for the Christian to focus on communion with God.

The strictness of the ascetics gave their teaching an added authority. The ascetics stressed deeds before words. Hard work in developing the inner life was far more important than obtaining a degree, writing a book, or being a skilled speaker. When one ascetic disciple admitted to his master that he had a secret desire to "acquire some taste and skill in words, so that I may reply more readily to those who question me," his master replied, "There is no need for that: the gift of speech, and indeed of silence, you may gain for yourself by purity of mind and heart."[18]

Ironically, this strictness with self was marked by a gentleness toward others. You see this in the historical accounts of the great ascetics. Martin of Tours, a late fourth-century ascetic, was said to be a person who neither judged nor condemned. Augustine wrote in *The City of God,* "What of those judgments passed by men on their fellow-men? What is our feeling about them? How pitiable, how lamentable do we find them!"[19] And Ambrose, also a well-known figure in the ascetic movement, was known to weep when he had to judge another Christian, "leaving a sound example to the priests who followed him, that they should rather intercede with God than bring charges against men."[20]

> *True ascetics are strict with themselves but treat others with supernatural gentleness.*

The legalism of the Pharisees caused them to set impossibly high standards that other people were obligated to follow, while the Pharisees basked in other luxuries. True ascetics are strict with themselves but treat others with supernatural gentleness.

Acts of Ascetics

Ascetics live in the three worlds of solitude, austerity, and strictness through various acts of devotion. The following discussion is by no means exhaustive, but it should prove helpful to get the ascetic temperament started on a productive and growing relationship with God.

Watching in the Night

It was a clear night; I held my recently fussy daughter in my arms, rocking her gently, side to side, looking out at the still neighborhood.

In the deep of the night, after even the late-night David Letterman crowd has gone to sleep, there is a stillness, an expectancy, a sense of waiting for the dawn to break open and overtake the darkness. Long after my daughter had drifted off to sleep, I wanted to stay awake.

Ascetics revel in this practice of quiet worship in the night. Many of us don't experience this except when a sick child forces us to be up late (or early), but some Christians have found the middle of the night to be one of their best times of prayer and worship.

Rather than staying up late, however, ascetics might try to rise earlier than normal, perhaps one day a week. If we do this on a weekend, we can go back to bed to catch up on lost sleep. "Missing sleep is not the important thing, though for some this can be a significant ascetical dimension of the practice," writes M. Basil Pennington, a twentieth-century monk.[21] Just as a teenager might shape her day in anticipation of a date or a sporting event, so as Christians we can reschedule a day in anticipation of time alone with God.

> Just as a teenager might shape her day in anticipation of a date or a sporting event, so as Christians we can reschedule a day in anticipation of time alone with God.

More important than losing sleep, Pennington continues, is being vigilant when others commonly are not. While others slumber, the ascetic lifts his or her soul to God; while all creation awaits the sun, the ascetic welcomes the Son.

Pennington tells us that this spirit of watching can be carried into the shower and the act of dressing, and remain with us throughout the day. Perhaps families can have agreements that once a week, or maybe once a month, radio, television, and unnecessary chatter before breakfast will not be allowed. Instead, there will be a holy stillness, an expectancy that invites the presence of God.

According to Pennington, it is hard to understand the value of such watching without actually doing it. "The value and effect of watching can only be known by experience," he writes.[22] Ascetics should certainly consider incorporating night watches into their regimen of worship.

I especially encourage people who struggle with insomnia to transform nights of frustration into great possibilities of prayer and worship. Many cases of insomnia can be directly related to stress, which intimate prayer and watching with the heavenly Father can ease.

Being Still

A friend of mine called to let me know he'd be in town, and would I like to meet for dinner? I'm always up for a dinner with him—he's a great conversationalist—so I readily agreed, and we went to a restaurant in the heart of the China district in Washington, D.C. We caught up on what each of us was doing, and my friend began telling me about a retreat he went to where they weren't allowed to speak for the first twenty-four hours.

Of all the types of retreats I could see my friend at, this wasn't one of them. "You've got to be kidding," I said. "What was it like?"

"At first, I hated it," he admitted. "I thought I was going to go crazy and this was going to be the longest weekend of my life. But you know, the next night they said we could talk for an hour or two, and by then, I didn't want to. I so enjoyed being quiet that talking seemed burdensome. I really enjoyed it."

Some monastic communities have become famous for their vows of silence, in which they agree to never speak again, or not speak for long periods of time. While this is not practical for many laypeople, we can appreciate some of the benefits of stillness by adopting it for shorter periods. Our needless chatter often dissipates our energy

If we give it time, however, most of us will not only grow comfortable with silence, but fond of it.

and scatters our thoughts from a focus on God. Trying to be silent for just a few hours will reveal how distracted we have become. At first, like my friend, we may hate being quiet. If we give it time, however, most of us will not only grow comfortable with silence, but fond of it.

Fasting

Benedictine monasteries were often considered "moderate" because their virtually perpetual fast (except during the Easter season, when fasting would be inappropriate) allowed one light meal a day. Like stillness, fasting reveals to us how much time and thought is taken up by transitory matters. Fasting can involve much more than food—we can fast from television, radio, movies, or certain types of food, desserts, meats, and the like.

The ascetic is willing to give up the "delights and consolations of this world"[23] so that he or she can enjoy the delights and consolations found in God. Renting a video to pass the weekend or turning on the radio to survive a commute can become habit-forming. To make sure these things aren't controlling us, we may need to give them up for a short period of time. The question I like to ask myself is, "Am I depending on this for spiritual nourishment?" If the answer is yes, I need to step back, or risk fostering a dependency.

Obeying

I had a close friend in college who actually drove at the speed limit of 55 miles an hour all the way from Bellingham to south of Seattle, a two- to three-hour drive (at that speed). When we were jogging together once through the middle of town, I suddenly noticed that I was alone. When I looked back, he was waiting for the traffic light to turn. There wasn't a car in sight, but if the sign said, "Wait," my friend was going to wait.

I've since lost track of my friend, so I have no idea if he has experienced the thrill of hurtling down a freeway at 62 miles an hour. Certainly, strict obedience can become legalistic; but on the other hand, I wonder if some of us haven't gone too far the other way.

Obedience was an important part of monastic living because it assaults our human pride and invites us to live in humility. While laypeople are not likely to enter into the strict obedience of a master/disciple relationship lived out in monastic times, we can still learn the blessing of obedience by obeying government authorities and employers; children can learn by obeying their parents.

I've been in a position of management in past years, and I've talked with other managers about the casualness with which people today are willing to cross the accepted lines of authority. One manager told me that a worker who was "temping" from an outside agency but hoping to secure full-time, permanent employment, blew his chances when he told the manager that he didn't like the way a decision was handled and expected the manager to justify his decision.

"I almost laughed," the manager said, "and managed to stifle the words I wanted to say, 'Who do you think cares about your opinion here? You're a temp!'"

That may sound harsh to some, but there's a truth underneath it all. It can be hard for all of us to "submit" and just accept someone else's leadership.

Leaders, bosses, and pastors are frequently second-guessed by people who have far less experience, far less information, and far less perspective than the one who is being questioned.

I know this may sound radical, but we live in a very arrogant society, fostered in part by the wrong notion that everybody's opinion is just as valid as anybody else's. This wrong notion is the child of relativism. We live in an age of polls and are encouraged to develop and publicize uninformed opinions. But there are some matters where my opinion is worth no more than a wild guess. It would be arrogant for me to seriously question someone who has a much better basis on which to form their opinion.

Without being legalistic, we need to realize that rebellion at any level can become habit-forming. If someone undermines the old boss, they are far more likely to do the same with the new boss. Respect for others is a matter of character and calls us to humility. It can take great humility to work under and submit to an imperfect human being, but that's what Scripture calls us to do. And if we're extremely cavalier about obeying legitimate earthly authorities, chances are we'll also be extremely lax about accepting God's authority. That's why we can learn so much by rediscovering the monastic emphasis on obedience.

An important point to remember is that ascetics practice obedience because this act is a way to honor God, not just because leaders are worthy to be obeyed. When government, parents, or employers direct us against the will of God, however, the first call of obedience is always to the will of God.

Working

It's startling to realize that Jesus was a common laborer for ninety percent of his life; just a very small amount of his time was spent in a visible, public ministry. Unless we want to accuse Jesus of being a poor steward of his time, we must reevaluate our distinction between secular and sacred work. Working hard is acceptable to God; done in the right spirit, it can be part of our worship to God. Benedict urged his monks to look at the tools of the monastery as if they were the vessels of the altar. "The monk in his labor is celebrating a liturgy, the liturgy of creation."[24]

Our lives take us through many different seasons and we must learn to adapt our spirituality and even our spiritual temperaments to meet the different demands of our changing life situations.

When we recognize that the strength and ability to work is God's gift to us to help us provide for our needs and the needs of our families, the use of that energy and skill becomes an affirmation of the God who created and sustains us. The plumber fixing a pipe under the sink, the construction worker driving a backhoe, and the pilot guiding a plane can all be worshiping God through their work. For ascetics, the harder the work, the better.

Taking Retreats

Limited retreats may be a mainstay of the ascetic's faith. Although modern ascetics may not live in complete solitude, they will still need to schedule time to be away for several hours, a day, or a week at a time. Apart from society, ascetics can then focus on drawing nearer to God.

Before my wife and I had kids, I planned a few overnight retreats. You can find monasteries within a few hours' drive, in many places. After the kids were born, extended time away became less possible. Besides, my work requires me to travel a great deal, so the last thing I want to do is consume another weekend.

Instead, I've discovered the value of "afternoon retreats." When I lived in Virginia, I slipped off to the National Cathedral in Washington, D.C., or spent a few hours hiking the Manassas, Virginia, battlefield. I don't get to do this as often as I would like now, or even as much as I think I need, but our lives take us through many different seasons and we must learn to adapt our spirituality and even our spiritual temperaments to meet the different demands of our changing life situations.

Living Simply

Ascetics will work to create simple living environments. On occasion, they may even create rooms that are especially reserved for prayer. Simplicity in dress and lifestyle may also be an important factor. Ascetics will avoid packed schedules and devotional rooms full of figurines.

If you're an ascetic, you may want to create a prayer room with bare, white walls and simple furniture. You'll likely prefer the quiet, so you'll need to find a place where noise won't be a problem. A silent, digital clock—or no clock at all—might be preferable to a clock with a moving hand that clicks each time the second hand moves. (If you don't understand the importance of this seemingly small detail—a quiet clock, for instance—you're not an ascetic; if you're smiling and saying, "Yes, of course," you may be!)

It's difficult for some Christians to understand, but the mere act of walking into such a barren and quiet room can call ascetics to worship just as an ornate Cathedral and the smell of incense can call sensate Christians.

Enduring Hardship

Serious training presupposes hardship. In a desire to draw near to God and take on God's character, ascetics embrace hardship rather than fight it.

An early Christian writer working under the pseudonym of Athanasius told of a (possibly fictional) account of a woman named Syncletica, whose story challenged many early Christians to endure hardship. This woman underwent severe physical pain, yet modeled great maturity o all those around her. When asked about this, Syncletica taught that we have an infantile and unpracticed soul. When sickness comes, the hardship we must endure can actually serve to strengthen us. "For just as the fetuses inside their mother, perfected from diminished food and life, and because of this are brought to a greater security; likewise the righteous withdraw from the ways of the world for the higher journey."

Early ascetics adopted practices like sleeping on the ground and exposing themselves to adverse weather conditions. Just like an Olympian runner might seek out the higher altitude of Denver, Colorado, so the ascetic might seek out harsher environments for his or her spiritual training.

In my own life, I have found that the demand to be warm when it is cold, and cool when it is hot reveals an infantile spiritual weakness. We want to be pampered. Years ago, when I worked in the fields as a boy harvesting rhubarb in the Pacific Northwest, I remember a Latin American field hand complaining to the American suburban kids he supervised: "In the morning you complain because the leaves are wet and make you cold; in the afternoon you complain because you're thirsty and it's too hot. How will you ever get any work done?"

> *When sickness comes, the hardship we must endure can actually serve to strengthen us.*

When sickness, heat, cold, hunger, or tiredness come—and they will—we can either adopt a demanding spirit and stunt our spiritual growth, or embrace them, learn from them, and mature in our faith. Our attitude will make all the difference.

The Temptations of Ascetics
Overemphasizing Personal Piety

In the book of Zechariah the people asked God if they should weep and fast as they had done for so many years. The Lord spoke through Zechariah, "Ask all the people of the land and the priests, 'When you fasted and mourned . . . was it really for me?'" Instead of outward displays of piety, God calls Israel to "administer true justice; show mercy and compassion to one another. Do not oppress the widow or the fatherless, the alien or the poor."[25]

The desire to seek solitude presents some problems since a full expression of Christianity requires an outward focus. Remember the limited role of the Nazirite—the vow was often taken with a definite end in sight. Jesus spent lengthy periods of prayer in solitude, but these were followed by public times of ministry. Jesus urged this same pattern—ministry followed by withdrawal and rest—on his disciples.[26] John the Baptist adopted the role of an ascetic, but this was also in preparation for a very public ministry.

> *It is futile to try to win God's approval or forgiveness by developing an extraordinary holiness.*

Our need for spiritual refreshment, then, must be balanced with our obligation to reach out to others.

Seeking Pain for Its Own Sake

Masochism is a sickness, not a spiritual path. Many of us in today's society are used to being pampered; we refuse even small discomfort and demand immediate relief. Others, however, through a distorted view of themselves or a diseased psyche, seek pain for its own sake. This is not the lesson of the ancient ascetics, nor is it a proper expression for the modern ones.

Healthy ascetics make it clear that asceticism is a means to an end. Whenever it becomes an end in itself, it is a gross distortion of a time-tested and treasured Christian practice.

Seeking to Gain God's Favor

The "heroic" measures of faith that the ascetic practices can become an attempt to gain God's favor. It is futile to try to win God's approval or forgiveness by developing an extraordinary holiness. We are so steeped in sin—attitudinal sins, like pride, as well as physical lusts of the flesh—that all our righteous acts are like filthy rags.[27]

We walk, live, and worship by faith in the completed work of Jesus Christ. Ascetics need to remember that fasting, sleeping on the ground, or living simply doesn't make God love us more. His love is absolute and his forgiveness is based on a prior work completed by Christ, not the spiritual experiences that we participate in today.

Are You an Ascetic?

Are you an ascetic? Score the following statements on a scale of five to one, with five being very true and one being not true at all. Record your answer in the space provided.

_____ 1. I feel closest to God when I am alone and there is nothing to distract me from focusing on his presence.

_____ 2. I would describe my faith as more "internal" than "external."

_____ 3. The words *silence, solitude,* and *discipline* are very appealing to me.

_____ 4. Taking an overnight retreat by myself at a monastery where I could spend large amounts of time alone in a small room, praying to God and studying his Word, and fasting for one or more days are all activites I would enjoy.

_____ 5. I would enjoy reading the book *A Place Apart: Monastic Prayer and Practice for Everyone.*

_____ 6. I would really enjoy spending time on a night watch, taking a short vow of silence, simplifying my life.

The total of all your answers. _____

Any score of fifteen or higher indicates a preference for this spiritual temperament.

Please take a moment now to register this score in chapter eleven on page 217 so you will have a composite picture of your soul's pathway to God.

An Invitation

Ascetics have an important lesson to teach the church and society. Seeking God entails some sort of separation from the world, even if that separation is expressed solely by inner detachment. The good-and-easy life lifted up by "Lifestyles of the Rich and Famous" and celebrity magazines often results in a poverty of spirit (just as forced poverty often results in a bitter spirit).

Ascetics testify to a higher life, a life of the spirit. This life is a high and holy invitation for those willing to take the road less traveled. A walk in the woods, intellectual challenge, enthusiastic celebration, active work for justice—all these have moved my spirit to some degree. But I've found that if the ascetic element of faith is completely lacking in my life, a spiritual bloatedness seeps in. Dietrich Bonhoeffer, the great German martyr and theologian, wrote that if we do not have some element of the ascetic in us, we will find it hard to follow Christ.

Ascetic practices keep us on the right track; they help us to move farther down the trail, regardless of what our main temperament may be.

SIX

ACTIVISTS:
LOVING GOD THROUGH
CONFRONTATION

Rob and I had spent the better part of the last hour in intense prayer. I don't know when I had felt closer to him. Together, we had played on the Puyallup city champion Little League baseball team. In high school, we graduated to the grueling cross-country runs—Rob having the advantage, I remember, of never needing to duck under low-lying branches. The respect, and even fear, for the impending pain before such races binds boys together like war binds men.

But now, in college, we were facing a new challenge. I don't know that either of us had ever been more nervous. Both Rob and I looked out over Red Square, shifting our weight from side to side; then, instinctively, we both knelt down to retie our shoes. Looking at each other, we laughed. Retying shoes is a natural habit for runners, but it was a classic case of symbolic nervous confusion for what we were about to be doing.

Rob laughed it off. "We don't want our shoes to fall off while we're preaching," he said.

The square started to fill with college students, and we both walked up to the fountain like two lightweights facing a boxing ring housing Muhammad Ali. We had done this before, but open-air preaching is never easy, especially to your collegiate peers.

Activists burst onto the history of faith in Scripture in both glory and infamy. It seems that few groups of believers can be so right at some times and so wrong at others.

Open-air preaching was probably my first introduction to the confrontational world of the activist. Emulated by many, yet scorned by an equal number, the activist is actually in good company, biblically speaking. This temperament of Christian can join such luminaries as Elijah and Moses, who both showed evidence of profound and courageous activism. From them and others we can learn both the blessings and pitfalls of loving God by standing up for righteousness.

Biblical Lessons of Activists

Activists burst onto the history of faith in Scripture in both glory and infamy. It seems that few groups of believers can be so right at some times and so wrong at others. When I think of Moses, Elijah, Habakkuk, and Peter, I think of men who have challenged me with their courage and leadership yet encouraged me through their weaknesses. Let's look at a few of these individuals to get a feel for the activist mentality.

Moses

Moses began his career as an activist (albeit a misguided one!) when he killed an Egyptian in defense of a fellow Israelite.[1] His strategy was all wrong, but he would need all that courage, and then some, in the years ahead. I've met few activists who don't cringe, as Moses must have, when they look back at their early days of faith.

It can take some time for the enthusiasm generated by the activist mentality to be tempered and seasoned by maturity and foresight.

Shortly thereafter, Moses the activist rescued some young women who were being pushed by unruly shepherds.[2] Whenever we see the young Moses, he's embroiled in confrontation.

It's somewhat of a surprise, then, that a little later in his life, Moses had to overcome a fearful reluctance when God wanted to bring him back into service. Moses seemed "gun-shy," as if his earlier experience shook his confidence and kept him from wanting to step forward one more time. Once he got moving, though, there was no stopping him. His example has been a great encouragement to me, for every activist must learn that faithful obedience doesn't always result in immediate success.

I think back to Moses' classic confrontation with Pharaoh. Moses didn't have the benefit of being told there would be ten plagues. All he knew was that God told him to tell Pharaoh, "Let my people go!" and that when he first obeyed, the situation actually grew worse. Pharaoh put a greater burden on the Israelites, and overnight Moses became the most hated man in Israel.

God sent Moses back again; and again, apart from a few snake tricks, nothing happened. It was at this point that the ten plagues *started*. I think most of us would quit around the third or fourth plague. I can just hear myself: "God, give me a break! I've done what you told me to do, five times now. Pharaoh hasn't set Israel free, so forget it. I'm done. Send somebody else."

Fortunately, Moses had been prepared. When God first gave Moses his commission, Moses answered, "Who am I, that I should . . . bring the Israelites out of Egypt?" God's response was an implicit rebuke against such self-sufficiency. He said simply, "I will be with you."[3] In other words, it doesn't matter who you are, Moses; what matters is who is sending you.

After great perseverance, Moses finally saw Israel go free. It wasn't long, however, before he adopted the "I'm the only one who can do it" complex and began wearing himself out on good causes.[4] Fortunately, Moses also had a teachable heart; by listening to his father-in-law he avoided the nervous exhaustion so common among activists. Still, his attitude reveals the danger of the activist mind-set, "Me and God against the world." At one point, Moses asked in desperation, "What am I to do with these people?"[5] Exasperation and fatigue are particular temptations for activist Christians.

Elijah and Elisha

Elijah's confrontations with the rulers of Israel rival Moses' confrontations with Pharaoh. Elijah displayed great courage in his confrontation with Ahab and the prophets of Baal, but his demeanor also reveals pride. Elijah thought he was the only true prophet left, and the only one who demonstrated true zeal.[6] However, God assured Elijah that seven thousand others were still true to the faith.

Elijah reveals classic activist symptoms (the negative kind) in his exhaustion and feelings of isolation.[7] Activism is one temperament that, while it tends to spiritually feed many Christians, can also exhaust them.

Elisha, Elijah's replacement, was also an activist, but showed great maturity in his confrontation with Hazael, who would eventually become King of Israel. Elisha saw the harm that Hazael would do and wept over it, but he didn't become consumed with it.[8] Most Christians have to learn that whenever God calls us to an activist posture, we must leave the results with him or we'll be consumed and driven by success rather than by the Holy Spirit. I've seen a number of activists who just can't accept defeat. When their political or social campaigns fail, their faith is rocked. Elisha would be a good character for such people to study, in part to keep them from responding like Habakkuk.

Habakkuk

Habakkuk is a good biblical warning to activists, one that I've taken to heart many times. I've heard too many prayers offered by activists in which God is accused more than he is petitioned, as if the activist is more concerned about justice than is God himself. Habakkuk cried out, "How long, O LORD, must I call for help, but you do not listen? Or cry out to you, 'Violence!' but you do not save? . . . Justice never prevails. The wicked hem in the righteous, so that justice is perverted."[9]

God's response to this accusation is instructive. He says that he is working behind the scenes. Justice is coming even though Habakkuk couldn't see it. Activists need to learn the message of the book of Habakkuk: live by faith.[10] Life situations and circumstances can tempt us to question God's sovereignty and goodness, but we see with a finite eye. God is not blind to injustice, nor is he indifferent.

The activist must be careful that intercession doesn't become accusation. Because there is so much apathy in our world, and even in the church, it is very easy for an activist to feel isolated and alone. We see the injustice, we see wickedness passed off as good, and our hearts burn within us, yet when we look around, the church seems to be sleeping. This can create an isolation that, if not kept in perspective, can eventually be broadened to include the "apathy" of God. Not only will the church not respond, the activist thinks, but even God is silent! When we think our concern for righteousness exceeds God's, we have slipped into the delusion of being self-appointed messiahs. "[The proud] is puffed up; his desires are not upright—but the righteous will live by his faith."[11]

> *I've heard too many prayers offered by activists in which God is accused more than he is petitioned, as if the activist is more concerned about justice than is God himself.*

Confrontation and Activists

A number of years ago, I heard of a local Christian activist who was circulating all the "ungodly" details of the movie *Back to the Future*. He had counted and listed all the offensive words, the number of times the Lord's name was taken in vain, and all the obscene gestures. As one of the leaders in a national network, I received his packet of information.

That guy should really get a life, I thought. *Of all the movies to attack.*

I had lunch with him after that, and he picked up the story again. I tried to display no emotion as he told me, "I went to several pastors and asked them if they had seen *Back to the Future*.

"'Sure,' they said. 'I took my kids.'

"'Did you walk out?'

"'No, of course not.'

"'Okay, could I have one minute during your worship service this week?' the man asked.

"'What for?' the pastors asked.

"'I want to read this list of words here, out loud. It shouldn't take more than a minute.'

"'There's absolutely no way I'd let you do that,' the pastors said."

The man's face grew grave as he looked me in the eyes and said, "I told them, 'How *dare* you take your kids to hear filth that you wouldn't want your adult congregation to hear.'"

The activist then went on to talk about Romans 12:9 which calls us to hate what is evil and cling to what is good.

"Do we really *hate* evil," he asked, "or are we content to put up with it?"

I hadn't taken my children to see that movie, but I left that lunch convicted nevertheless. I sensed a growing coldness in my heart. Most of the time, I may resist evil, but do I really hate it?

The sad truth is, not always.

The lunch with that activist was anything but "pleasant." In fact, it was rather exhausting. But this man was responsible for ridding a good part of northern Virginia from certain types of pornography, and he's had a major role in activating the church to reach out to prisoners and to take a more active role opposing abortion, and I needed to hear what he had to say.

He told me that he and his wife don't get invited to dinner very often, and talking to him, I could see why. If he sees or hears of something that is wrong, he's going to address it, confront it, and force you to take a second look at it. He's a gadfly.

I wouldn't do everything the same way this man does—I can't imagine going from church to church, talking to pastors about taking their kids to see *Back to the Future*—but the same God who created bunnies and gadflies created contemplatives and activists. This man is fed by righteous confrontation. You can see it in his eyes. He's not going to run from a fight.

No, I wouldn't want everybody in the church to behave the way he does, but I certainly wouldn't want everyone in the church to behave the way I do, either.

Activists, you see, are actually spiritually nourished through the battle, which is not such a bad thing. Jesus himself said, "My food . . . is to do the will of him who sent me and to finish his work."[12] And like it or not, much of Jesus' work involved intense confrontation with the Pharisees.

Of course, the *way* we do God's work will determine whether or not we are being fed.

Many years ago, Francis Schaeffer wrote in *The Mark of the Christian,* "There is only one kind of person who can fight the Lord's battles in anywhere near a proper way, and that is the person who by nature is unbelligerent. A belligerent person tends to do it because he or she is belligerent; at

> *Activists . . . are actually spiritually nourished through the battle.*

least it looks that way. The world must observe that, when we must differ with each other as true Christians, we do it not because we love the smell of blood, the smell of the arena, the smell of the bullfight, but because we must for God's sake."[13]

Thus the example of Moses, the "reluctant activist," is particularly appropriate. When activists live to see justice and righteousness worked out so that it is visibly evident in the church and in society, and they do this as a way of loving God, the confrontation will actually bring fulfillment, not exhaustion; thanksgiving, not anger; and often a deeper sense of intimacy with God rather than a deeper sense of self-righteousness.

I found this to be especially true in my open-air preaching days. Temptations abound on a college campus. Tight accountability groups can help, but nothing was more effective to banning the lure of temptation than knowing I'd be preaching the next morning.

It was like training for a big race. Having something to look forward to gave me reason to forgo other activities. The fear involved in confrontation creates a certain dependence on God that isn't normally there. You don't just love him, you need him—desperately. Your primary fear is that he'll leave and you'll be left to face the challenge on your own.

Facing this fear and stepping out in faith, and finding God faithful as he steps in to carry you, can do wonders for your intimacy with God. You appreciate him more. I've found that facing a trial with God builds fellowship with him no less than does facing a trial with a fellow human being.

In defense of their work, activists may frequently cite Jesus' cleansing of the temple. Jesus did more than heal, activists say. He also confronted. He was holy, which is something very different from nice. In *The Mark of the Christian*, Francis Schaeffer wrote, "So often people think that Christianity is only something soft, only a kind of gooey love that loves evil equally with good. This is not the biblical position. The holiness of God is to be exhibited simultaneously with love."[14]

> *The fear involved in confrontation creates a certain dependence on God that isn't normally there. You don't just love him, you need him—desperately.*

It is this fear of confrontation that keeps many from becoming activists. As soon as you take a stand, you'll be shot at. I'll always remember the first time in college that a leader of a proabortion group wrote a particularly biting letter to the editor in which I was attacked. It wasn't easy. In junior high, I was voted "most polite," and it took some time for me to realize that being perceived as a "nice guy" and being a faithful Christian don't always go hand in hand.

On another occasion, when I was working as a campus pastor, I met with the leader of a campus gay-rights group. This leader used to attend a Christian group, and I was hoping to win him back to the faith. First, I wanted to listen and find out what was driving him, so I asked him what the goals of his group were. He looked into my eyes and said with startling dispassion, "To undo everything you guys are trying to do."

I realized then that my desire to be "liked" had to be crucified. I never want to be patently offensive or stupidly obnoxious, but the fact is, some people have chosen to hate God and his kingdom. If I am going to identify myself with God and his kingdom, I will be hated as well. We can't expect to faithfully serve God and be liked by his enemies.

My activism has resulted more from obedience than temperament; I don't consider myself an activist at heart, and I scored very low on this temperament in the test at the end of this book. I've been challenged to be proactive, however, by passages such as Proverbs 24:11–12: "Rescue those being led away to death; hold back those staggering toward slaughter. If you say, 'But we knew nothing about this,' does not he who weighs the heart perceive it? Does not he who guards your life know it? Will he not repay each person according to what he has done?" Other passages of Scripture that speak to the heart of the activist include Psalms 7, 68, and 140, and Ezekiel 33:1–20.

I have witnessed an irony in this temperament, however. While activism and even confrontation feed many Christians, they can also leave us depleted. Elijah is a classic case study for this. If activists notice a tendency toward isolation and accusation, they would do well to consider whether they have lost their balance. This is why activists must find other ways to supplement their spiritual nourishment.

After Jesus' disciples confronted the powers of Satan, Jesus insisted that they get some rest. Without rest, activists may adopt the self-defeating motivations of hatred and anger instead of love and compassion. Activists need to find the right balance—indeed, the balance modeled by Christ who regularly interspersed times of spiritual refreshment with intense ministry.

I've also found it helpful to try and turn my activism into spiritual intimacy. How? Thomas Merton provides a clue when he suggests that activists can actually enjoy a "masked" contemplation if we're active for the right reasons. Some Christians have tried to drive a wedge between an activist and a contemplative calling. Certainly both temperaments display their differences, but Merton found that at least a certain synthesis could be reached.

There are many Christians who serve God with great purity of soul and perfect self-sacrifice in the active life. Their vocation does not allow them to find the solitude and silence and leisure in which to empty their minds entirely of created things and to lose themselves in God alone. They are too busy serving Him in His children on earth. At the same time, their minds and temperaments do not fit them for a purely contemplative life: they would know no peace without exterior activity.... Nevertheless they know how to find God by devoting themselves to Him in self-sacrificing labors in which they are able to remain in His presence all day long.... Although they are active laborers they are also quasi-contemplatives because of their great purity of heart maintained in them by obedience, fraternal charity, self sacrifice and perfect abandonment to God's will in all that they do and suffer. They are much closer to God than they realize. They enjoy a kind of "masked" contemplation.[15]

> *When our activism is oriented around the love of God, it is as acceptable to God as the contemplative's prayer. If it is oriented around confrontation for its own sake, we may be feeding a sinfully divisive spirit rather than serving the unifying Holy Spirit.*

Merton stresses, however, that there is a great difference between "quasi-contemplatives" and those whose Christian life is mere piety and routine. The difference is that the true Christian activist "lives for God and for his love alone." When our activism is oriented around the love of God, it is as acceptable to God as the contemplative's prayer. If it is oriented around confrontation for its own sake, we may be feeding a sinfully divisive spirit rather than serving the unifying Holy Spirit.

Forms of Activism

Activism can take many forms. Frank Schaeffer (the son of Francis Schaeffer) argues for an activist-oriented "literature of Christian resistance" in which Christians of all traditions vigorously defend true Christianity and its beliefs.[16] As a writer, I'm pleased to see that there is, indeed, a strong tradition of Christian pamphleteering and publishing that confront failures and lapses both within and without the church. The late Dr. Klaus Bockmuehl wrote a small but seminal piece in this regard entitled *Books: God's Tools in the History of Salvation*.[17] When Abraham Lincoln met Harriet Beecher Stowe, author of *Uncle Tom's Cabin*, he quipped, "So this is the woman who started the [civil] war." In the nineteenth century, Charles Dickens pled the case of the London orphaned while Tolstoy passionately portrayed the downtrodden. In the twentieth century, Richard Wright, in his novel *Black Boy*, opened many eyes to the difficulties of growing up as a minority in rural Mississippi while C. S. Lewis wrote his popular Narnia series as "a sort of pre-baptism of the child's imagination." These and many other writers have changed the destinies of millions through the written word.

Another form of activism is working for social reform. John Wesley wrote that there is "no holiness but social holiness ... and to turn Christianity into a solitary religion is to destroy it."[18] Charles Finney refused to baptize Christians who still believed in slavery while William Wilberforce fought slavery in his own country, England. The Christian church has often led the way in societal reform, today fighting the evils of abortion and child pornography, among others.

I worked a number of years for a pro-life organization, and one of the most difficult challenges I've faced is helping other Christians adopt this sense of social responsibility. Too often we think that as long as we attend church regularly, tithe from our income, and don't willingly live in sin, we've done our Christian duty. Yet the Bible is filled with calls for God's people to reach out to the less fortunate (James 1:27; Matthew 25:35–36; and others).

There is a tension in this, however. Good Christian minds disagree on many issues, such as school prayer, the government's use of welfare, and capital punishment, to name just a few examples. While we may find Christian brothers and sisters advocating an opposing position, as Christians and as citizens we have a responsibility to be first, fully informed; second, prayerfully decisive; and third, fully involved.

Activism can also call us to not just work for social reform, but also actively confront error and evil. The late Francis Schaeffer wrote that sometimes "truth equals confrontation." His son, Frank Schaeffer, warns that we must therefore be willing to challenge and answer the enemies of the truth. This is by nature a confrontational work. "Those who wish to join in the ecumenism of orthodoxy cannot be a silent majority. We must be an aggressive, feisty, dig-in-your-heels, kick-and-scream bunch; we must work twice as hard because there are fewer of us."[19]

Writers, preachers, politicians, academics, artists, and home-makers can all be activists, faithful in their own sphere to stand up for the truth. Frank Schaeffer argues that Christians should be open to new ideas but actively mold events in the arena of education, ideology, the electoral process, the national agenda, protest, the media, waywardness in the church, and strengthening the family—

Activists will never be satisfied playing it safe. They need to experience the exhilaration of seeing a miraculous God come through in miraculous ways.

beginning with our own.[20] In this, Christian activism can move beyond protest to provide a positive alternative. Instead of just writing letters to Congress, Christians can run for Congress. Instead of protesting immorality in entertainment, Christians can become part of the entertainment industry.

On a more individual basis, I've witnessed that activists, by temperament, have an acute need for "spiritual risk-taking." While the rest of us prefer to play it safe, activists often exhibit an almost insatiable need to see God break through in mighty ways. These are the men and women who found nonprofit organizations on twenty-five dollars and prayer, who eagerly begin national campaigns against systemic evil, and who achieve what others said could never be done.

Activists will never be satisfied playing it safe. They need to experience the exhilaration of seeing a miraculous God come through in miraculous ways. In this sense, the activist frequently bears some resemblance to the enthusiast.

Prayer and Activists

If ever there was a group I would want to see plugged into prayer, it would be the activists. Fortunately, many of the activists I know regularly participate in various forms of prayer.

Walking Prayer

Many activists may find that "walking prayer" is particularly helpful. The evangelist might intercede for a city block by walking around it as he prays silently; the intercessor might walk around a government building while she prays for justice. Some Christians have been known to circle an abortion clinic or a hospital. Others will spread a map in front of them and pray for unreached people groups.

Processions

"Jesus" marches, in which large numbers of Christians gather to march in celebration of Jesus, are making a surprising comeback. I say "comeback" because an ancestral practice can be found going back as far as the Baroque period (roughly 1550–1750). Today's marches are somewhat different, as they focus more on praise and celebration, whereas the earlier community marches tended to seek some spiritual favor and were frequently very solemn affairs. They became so common that A. L. Mayer has called the Baroque period the Age of Processions.[21]

Intercession

Karl Barth urged Christians to pray with the Bible in one hand and a newspaper in the other. Intercession can definitely be considered a form of Christian activism, and not just for political ends. I remember rising early once a week in college to attend missions prayer meetings. We didn't bring a newspaper with us, but we did carry materials prepared from various missions groups. Such meetings still take place in many churches, often on Sunday evenings.

Prayer should be an important part of the life of the activist. Work as prayer is important and valid, but coming away to pray is also important. Activists, by nature led to confront and face evil and injustice on a regular basis, need prayer to stay focused and unpolluted. Hatred for sin can become hatred for people when activists become tired and spiritually depleted. Before long, unprayerful activists begin to take apathy personally and can begin alienating most Christians around them. If you're an activist, do yourself and the church a favor: cultivate an active prayer life.

> *Activists . . . need prayer to stay focused and unpolluted. Hatred for sin can become hatred for people when activists becomes tired and spiritually depleted.*

The Temptations of Activists

Becoming Judgmental

Activists might think that the holier they become, the more they will hate sin. This is true. Where activists often go wrong, however, is making the leap in logic to assume that the holier they become, the less able they will be able to tolerate sinners. This is clearly not true.

As a student of the Christian classics, I've found most spiritual writers agree that as we mature in our faith, we become more eager to see sin leave our lives, yet more compassionate toward other sinners. Our love, as well as our holy hatred of sin, should grow. A self-righteous, critical attitude is not a reflection of the compassion of Christ. Activists may see far too few Christians really hating the sin and overcompensate by forgetting to love the sinner.

Those who take up arms to kill abortion doctors, for instance, betray the very cause they seek to serve. I thank God no one killed Bernard Nathanson (a former abortionist) or Carol Everett (a former abortion clinic owner) or Norma McCorvey (a.k.a. Jane Roe of *Roe vs. Wade*), as these three have become articulate defenders of life. I'm also thankful early Christians didn't assassinate Saul, who actively persecuted and murdered Christians, before he became the apostle Paul. Through history and Scripture we learn that we must do God's work *in God's way*.

Ambition and Sex

I'm going out on a limb on this one. But from personal observation and being a student of biography, there seems to be a direct spiritual relationship between the level of a person's ambition and sexual temptation, especially in men. The stories of Christian men who have accomplished a great deal but fallen into sexual immorality are so numerous I don't need to recount them.

At its deepest root, ambition is often a fight against powerlessness and a fight for control. The ambitious person is also inherently selfish. This search for control, unimpeded by thoughts of concern for another's welfare, certainly provide a fertile seedbed for sexual lust, which may therefore find a particularly comfortable home in an ambitious soul.

I was speaking to a group of Christian activists not that long ago, and I sobered them with the words, "The very qualities that help you succeed as an activist may tempt you to fail as a Christian."

Ambitious men and women need to allow others to hold them accountable. Ambition coupled with secrecy is a fertile ground for sexual sin; throw in fatigue, and you're almost certain to embarrass yourself and the ministry God has given you. The activist may face more temptation in this regard than many of the other temperaments.

Elitism and Resentment

Because the activist is fed by confrontation, he or she may not understand why others fear it so much. Even the thought of a picket or contact evangelism may be debilitating to some, while very exciting to others. This can produce an elitist attitude.

A good warning is found in 1 Samuel 30. During one of David's battles, many of the soldiers grew tired during a desperate chase, so David left them to watch the supplies while he and the others went off to complete the conflict. Among the men who continued the chase and returned victorious, an elitist attitude arose: "Because they did not go out with us, we will not share with them the plunder we have recovered," they said.[22]

David, fortunately, stepped in. "No, my brothers, you must not do that with what the LORD has given us. He has protected us and handed over to us the forces that came against us."[23] Notice what David is saying. Paraphrased, it's this: "You're forgetting something, men. God, not our own strength, gave us this victory so everyone is going to share."

David made this a statute and an ordinance: The one who fights and the one who guards the supplies will receive the same reward. This mirrors the apostle Paul's numerous statements about respecting different spiritual gifts and callings.

Preoccupation with Activity and Statistics

When a young child is frustrated with a toy that is stuck in something or a knot that won't come undone, she may respond by just trying harder, often making the situation worse. Sincerity and effort are two strong legs, but two legs are not enough to stabilize a stool. Christian activists need sincerity, effort, *and* thoughtful prayer.

A minister who had misgivings about the prohibition movement remarked that "the churches in the long run would get further if their activities were marked by less commotion and more insight."[24] It is hard to disagree with this. Jesus, as always, is the perfect model of a man who worked hard during the day and prayed hard during the morning and night. Peter is the model of a man who acted fast (cutting off a soldier's ear, for instance) and had much to repent.

Lack of Emphasis on Personal Sanctity

Jesus was very clear that we are to remove the log from our own eye before we reach for the splinter in our neighbor's eye.[25] Societal reform begins with the individual who is seeking to reform society. Social action can never be a substitute for personal sanctity. In fact, social action without personal sanctity can do as much harm as good: it discredits the cause if we are found to be a hypocrite.

Are You an Activist?

Are you an activist? Score the following statements on a scale of five to one, with five being very true and one being not true at all. Record your answer in the space provided.

_____ 1. I feel closest to God when I'm cooperating with him in standing up for his justice: writing letters to government officials and newspaper editors, picketing at an abortion clinic, urging people to vote, or becoming familiar with current issues.

_____ 2. I get very frustrated if I see apathetic Christians who don't become active. I want to drop everything else I'm doing and help the church overcome its apathy.

_____ 3. The words *courageous confrontation* and *social activism* are very appealing to me.

_____ 4. Activities like confronting a social evil, attending a meeting to challenge the new curriculum before the local school board, and volunteering on a political campaign are important to me.

_____ 5. The book written by Frank Schaeffer, *A Time for Anger,* would be an important book for me to read.

_____ 6. I would like to awaken the church from its apathy.

The total of all your answers. _____

Any score of fifteen or higher indicates a preference for this spiritual temperament. Record your score in chapter eleven on page 217 so you will have a composite picture of your soul's path to God.

A High Calling

Although I don't consider myself an activist at heart, I have a great deal of respect for activists' role in the church and the world. A strong ego is often necessary because the activist is frequently ostracized from the rest of the community. Most Christians I know would absolutely wilt if a newspaper article publicly belittled them. The activist just seems to smile, appreciate the photo, and move on.

This can become prideful, and at that point it needs to be dealt with, but I'm frequently reminded that our God is in the business of using imperfect people, even transforming character flaws into useful tools and strengths.

The church has frequently had an uneasy relationship with activists and prophets. We fondly remember those who have died but often loathe those who are still living. This should lead the activist to love God all the more, because God may frequently be his or her only friend! Being an activist is a high calling, but it needs to be done with the right motivation. Calling activism a "sacred pathway" should help: We're active because that's the best way for us to express our love for God. Armed with this attitude, a successful ministry (rather than a personal monument) will soon follow.

> *The church has frequently had an uneasy relationship with activists and prophets. We fondly remember those who have died but often loathe those who are still living*

SEVEN

CAREGIVERS: LOVING GOD BY LOVING OTHERS

"Gary, I need some help."

I winced. I knew what was coming, but I didn't want to hear it. Gordy moved his wheelchair a little closer and whispered, "I had a little accident."

"Sure, no problem, Gord," I answered. "Let's go take care of it."

Gordy attended the same university as I, but he was in the advanced stages of muscular dystrophy. He was just two years away from dying of pneumonia, which frequently ends the lives of those suffering from MD. As Gordy's condition worsened, his need for extra help increased. I had seen another Christian taking care of him just a week before during a different bout of diarrhea and remembered saying to myself, "I couldn't do that." I was about to find out differently.

Gordy was more familiar with the situation than I, and we were actually able to enjoy ourselves through the whole experience. Since I had been duly "initiated," I also became one Gordy could, and did, frequently call on when his paid person wasn't available.

You remember the silliest things. Once I took his shirt off and was folding it when I heard this very patient but very urgent, "Gary!" I turned and caught Gordy before he fell all the way back. Gordy laughed, and I laughed, and the next time I remembered to prop him up with my knees while I pulled his shirt over his head.

Of all the things, I remember his feet the most. They showed all the signs of never being used. Gordy had been unable to walk for ten years by the time I met him, and he wore slippers instead of shoes. In our privatized world, I've met very few people who don't admit to some insecurity about their feet. Footwashings, commemorating Christ's work at the Last Supper, are enough to keep many of us from church. But Gordy was silent. He knew I would see everything, but he said nothing.

> Gordy's outward disability became, in a very real sense, my inward cure. His willingness to let another see his weakness revealed an inspiring inner strength.

It was as I was putting on his socks one day that I realized Gordy was the holy one in all our efforts. He was serving me, and in some very practical ways, sacrificing the privacy of his body to do it. I was so disabled inside, afraid to let people see my faults and struggles, because my disabilities could be hidden. Gordy's outward disability became, in a very real sense, my inward cure. His willingness to let another see his weakness revealed an inspiring inner strength.

One Saturday morning, I awoke early and made my way to the men's bathroom. As is not uncommon in a college dorm, someone had had too much to drink the night before and hadn't been able to make it to the toilet. The one handicapped stall was covered with vomit—the mess was on the floor, the toilet bowl, everywhere.

Normally, I would have shaken my head in disgust and moved on, but an inner prompting wouldn't let me do it. Gordy couldn't just move on. The cleaning person wouldn't be in until Monday, and this was the only bathroom Gordy could use. I had helped Gordy many times before when he had seen me, but this was a time when he needed me, but wouldn't know it and wouldn't see it.

I shuffled back to the sinks, wet some paper towels, and went to work. Fifteen, maybe twenty minutes later, it was done. Gordy never knew. His weekend went on as usual, the sound of his chair whizzing down the hallway continued unabated, but I was changed. Gordy's life had touched me again. Something moved inside me and I realized, not in an idealized way, but with full understanding, why many monks often considered disabled people especially holy. The lessons they can teach us are profound.

Mother Teresa of Calcutta looked behind the eyes of the poor, the sick, and the needy, and said she saw the image of God. She learned to love God by loving others. Such a statement may put the "codependency police" on red alert, but psychological maladies aside, many people have found that one of the most profound ways we can love God is to love

> *For caregivers, giving care isn't a chore but a form of worship.*

others. For caregivers, giving care isn't a chore but a form of worship. I've heard that Mother Teresa asked all prospective oblates, "Does your work give you joy?" If the answer was "No," they didn't make it in.

Martyrs need not apply.

Biblical Examples of Caregivers

Caregivers can look to two people in particular as they seek to understand their calling and temperament: Mordecai and Jesus.

Mordecai

The portrait painted of Mordecai in the book of Esther is the portrait of a man who deeply and profoundly cares about others and freely pours out his energy to help them. The first picture we have of Mordecai is in Esther 2:7 where we learn that he raised Esther after she was orphaned by a forced relocation of her parents. "Mordecai had taken her as his own daughter when her father and mother died."

Mordecai's effort on Esther's behalf was tremendous. Even after she was taken into the palace, he remained intimately involved and concerned over her welfare. "Every day he walked back and forth near the courtyard of the harem to find out how Esther was and what was happening to her."[1]

A less concerned man might simply have washed his hands of her. He had done his duty, after all, taking her in; but now she was gone, so couldn't he just forget about her and attend to the rest of his business? A lesser man, maybe, but not Mordecai.

The second picture we are given of Mordecai occurs later in the second chapter. This time, Mordecai was looking after the king. He overheard two of the king's servants plot to harm the king. Mordecai reported what he heard and saved the king from harm. In just two chapters, Mordecai has provided for an orphan and protected a king.

Mordecai was not a people pleaser, however, and this removes our suspicions of "codependency." We learn in chapter three that he incurred the wrath of Haman because he refused to bow down in Haman's presence. Mordecai served others when he could serve God by doing so. When the two came in conflict, Mordecai pleased God.

Not only did Mordecai care for an orphan and for the king, he also cared for an entire race, the Jewish people. When Haman retaliated against Mordecai by obtaining permission to wipe out the Jews, Mordecai "tore his clothes, put on sackcloth and ashes, and went out into the city, wailing loudly and bitterly."[2]

By undergoing such humiliation and discomfort, Mordecai was able to communicate the urgency of Israel's danger to Esther, who finally dispatched a servant to find out what was going on. When Esther balked at the only route of escape, Mordecai stood firm. "Do not think that because you are in the king's house you alone of all the Jews will escape.... And who knows but that you have come to royal position for such a time as this?"[3]

It has always amazed me how true caregivers—shepherds—can become lions if need be to carry out their mission. Though a caregiver, Mordecai was obviously not a weak man. He could be forceful, even with those he loved deeply, when circumstances insisted that he be firm.

It's worth noting that if Mordecai had refused to care for the orphaned Esther, all Israel might have been lost, for Mordecai would have had no way to reach the king. His earlier act of care provided the opportunity for a later act of care, one on a far broader scale.

Through Mordecai's insistence, God's providence provided a way for Israel to defend itself. Again Mordecai was the primary caregiver here, carefully writing out instructions to his fellow Israelites that were sent to all surrounding provinces so the Israelites would know how to defend themselves.[4]

Once Israel was victorious, Mordecai's caregiving continued. He established a yearly festival to celebrate God's protection and intervention. He could easily have established a monument to his own faithfulness, but instead he decreed that the Israelites celebrate by sending presents to one another and by giving gifts to the poor. Rather than thinking of himself, Mordecai invented new ways to care for those in need.[5]

At all points, Mordecai was looking after others: first an orphan, then a king, then a nation, then the poor. His epitaph, the last verse in Esther, is fitting: "Mordecai the Jew was second in rank to King Xerxes, preeminent among the Jews, and held in high esteem by his many fellow Jews, because he worked for the good of his people and spoke up for the welfare of all the Jews."[6]

Who could hope for a more notable epitaph?

Jesus

Because he was the only truly whole man who ever lived, Jesus displayed all the spiritual temperaments we discuss. We, more fragmented and broken, lack the depth and breadth revealed in the life of Christ. Jesus' life particularly shines, however, in the area of being a consummate caregiver. Jesus cared for the sick, the demon-possessed, and the lost. He urged his followers to give to the poor, and he had great compassion on the multitudes.[7]

While many people assume that "religion" and caring for others go hand in hand, it is only because of Jesus that this is so. He is most responsible among religious leaders for associating love for God with love for others—particularly the downtrodden. Islam was founded in warfare and has a confrontational edge to its message (though, admittedly, of the "five obligations," one is to give one-fortieth—2.5%—of your income to the poor); the morality of Buddhism is based on refraining from evil, not alleviating the suffering of others (since suffering, in Buddhist thought, is an illusion anyway); and Hindus are concerned with avoiding negative karma and thereby escaping from the wheel of life, death, and rebirth.

Entwining love for God with love for others and adopting a "positive" morality ("Do unto others as you would have them do unto you") rather than a negative one ("Don't do unto others what you don't want them to do unto you") was a rather radical message in Jesus' day—an expansion of Old Testament, Jewish-based calls for social mercy. The spread of Christ's message is the main reason that people today assume religion and caring should be intricately interwoven.

> While many people assume that "religion" and caring for others go hand in hand, it is only because of Jesus that this is so.

One picture in particular reveals the caregiving heart of Jesus. When he heard that John the Baptist had been beheaded, Jesus knew his earthly ministry had taken a serious turn toward Calvary—a long, torturous, and bloody death was now in his near future. And before that ordeal, he had to make sure that a group of unruly disciples could be trained to carry on his message once he was gone. If ever a man deserved solitude, it was Jesus. If ever there was a time to set legitimate limits—to pray and process all that was happening—this was it.

The needy and insatiable crowds followed, however. Imagine an ice cream man walking into a group of hungry kids clawing and grabbing at his clothes. That's what it must have felt like for Jesus to look out and see that the crowds still wanted more. Yet when Jesus saw them "he had compassion on them and healed their sick."[8]

Incredibly, Jesus' ministry continued for several hours. Jesus, still tired, still deep in thought about the seriousness of the day's events, continued to give, to heal, and to teach. The crowds were there long enough to grow hungry—providing a great excuse, the disciples thought, to get rid of the people. Remember, Jesus wasn't the only one who was tired, his disciples must have been tired, too. There was likely more than a little self-interest in their voices when they said, "Come on, Jesus, the people are hungry. Isn't it time to send them away?"

Hypocritical compassion. The disciples wanted peace, rest, and quiet for themselves, but pretended to care about the crowds. Jesus, full of the caregiver's heart, looked at them and said, "They do not need to go away. You give them something to eat."

I can see the furrowed brows. I can imagine the disciples' calculations: "If we have to feed this lot, we're talking days of gathering and preparation, days before we can rest! Days before we can eat in peace! Surely he can't mean that!" So they pull out the trump card.

"We have here only five loaves of bread and two fish." Enough for the disciples, maybe, but certainly not thousands of people.

Jesus was undoubtedly hungry himself. Clothed in the incarnation, he was subject to weariness, hunger pangs, and physical exhaustion. Producing great miracles must have been physically painful and very tiring, certainly much more taxing than merely snapping his fingers and watching everything move. Still, Jesus exerted himself once more, performed yet another miracle—this one on the perimeter of exhaustion—and fed the people, again sacrificing his own needs of rest and refreshment before sending them away.

That Jesus needed time alone is emphasized by his movements once the crowd was fed. Matthew tells us, "Immediately Jesus made the disciples get into the boat and go on ahead of him to the other side, while he dismissed the crowd. After he had dismissed them, he went up on a mountainside by himself to pray."

Jesus placed his own needs under the needs of others. He had a more important mission to accomplish than anyone who has

Attending to "spiritual concerns" is not an excuse for refusing to get our hands dirty.

ever lived, yet he still found time to care for the basic needs of a sick, hungry, and unruly crowd. This example continues to challenge me today. It is so easy to ignore the needs of others around us because we have "more important things" to do, but Jesus defined those very needs as a central part of our mission. I don't need to quote the entire parable of the Good Samaritan for us to be reminded that attending to "spiritual concerns" is not an excuse for refusing to get our hands dirty.

Biblical Exhortations of Caregiving

The biblical challenges to love God by caring for others are legion. The story of the Good Samaritan is probably one of the most popular parables in the entire New Testament. As we mentioned earlier, its meaning is clear. Nobody is so important or so wise that they can excuse themselves from practical helps. Jesus emphasized compassion in so many of his teachings that it's no surprise his disciples, the New Testament writers, also urge us to love God this way.

John tells us that "we know that we have passed from death to life, because we love our brothers."[9] In fact, lack of love for others calls into question whether we love God at all. "If anyone has material possessions and sees his brother in need but has no pity on him, how can the love of God be in him?"[10]

Paul joins John in urging Christians to look after others: "Each of you should look not only to your own interests, but also to the interests of others."[11] The writer of Hebrews equates loving others with loving God: "God is not unjust; he will not forget your work and the love you have shown him as you helped his people and continue to help them."[12] Later, this same writer reminds believers that in giving care to strangers, we may actually be entertaining angels.[13]

James says that "pure and faultless" religion is looking after orphans and widows in their distress.[14] Peter urges us to be hospitable and to use whatever gift God has given us to minister to one another.[15]

The breadth of this teaching and the fact that it is repeated by so many writers of the New Testament leave us without any doubt as to the importance of loving God by loving those he has made. Though some people excel in this avenue of loving God, it should be a part of every Christian's life.

One verse in particular has greatly challenged me. The afternoon that its truth gripped me is one I won't soon forget. The city of Sodom is often alluded to in Christian circles as *the* wicked city, but what really was Sodom's gravest sin? Listen to Ezekiel: "Now this was the sin of your sister Sodom: She and her daughters were arrogant, overfed and unconcerned; they did not help the poor and needy."[16]

I definitely have plenty of pride in my life. On a worldwide scale, I am certainly "overfed." I also have to own up to an attitude of "unconcern." These three things being true, the only thing keeping me from the sin of Sodom, the biblical picture of wickedness at its basest form, is whether or not I am "helping the poor and needy."

We like to define holiness by avoiding transgression, but in God's book, the sin of omission (not doing what we should do) ranks right up there with the sin of commission (doing something we shouldn't do).

Patterns of Caregiving

I have great admiration for those who have taken on the task of caring for others in need. I remember a campus ministry intern who lived in an apartment building that I managed when I was going to seminary. Two deeply troubled men moved in next door to him.

If it wasn't drugs, it was alcohol. Several nights a week, the intern would find one of his neighbors mumbling unintelligible words or passed out in the hallway. He'd pick them up, pack them into his car, and take them to the detoxification center. (If you've never transported an intoxicated person before, you may not be able to appreciate the risk of using your own car for this purpose.)

When the intern finally received a call to a ministry out-of-state, he told the good news to his neighbors. "Hey," they said, "who's gonna take us to detox when we mess up?"

More recently, I heard the testimony of a remarkable couple who have taken a severely brain-damaged infant into foster care. Gail Kelley and her husband told the story of Manuel, short for "Emmanuel," a severely disabled foster son who was the result of an incestuous relationship and who was further damaged in utero by a poorly prescribed drug. One night, Gail was up late with Manuel as he suffered repeated seizures. Each seizure activity was destroying more brain cells, and Gail's tears wet Manuel's black hair as she realized Manuel didn't have all that many brain cells left to lose.

A three-minute seizure at 3:30 A.M. began a horrifying ordeal. A two-and-one-half-minute seizure hit at 3:34. A frightfully long seizure, lasting a full five minutes, occurred at 3:44. A few minutes later, at 3:56, another three-minute seizure took hold.

Each time, exaggerated spastic movements took control over Manuel's arms. At first his legs were stiff and rigid, until they, too, began to shake and quiver. Manuel's head flinched and jerked out of control. His left eye alternatively closed, then bounced in all directions, while his right eye rhythmically vibrated. At times, Manuel would choke, or saliva would drip from the left corner of his mouth. Then, as the seizure came to an end, Manuel's tongue would gently quiver, drawing slightly backwards, and the seizure would be like two giant arms that gently laid him to rest.

Two more seizures took hold, one at 4:00 A.M. and another at 4:20. Spent, exhausted, frightened, and depleted, Gail began crying uncontrollably. She was afraid that Manuel would soon die in her arms, so she pleaded with God, "I haven't had enough time with him. Please, God, don't take him from me now."

Gail "heard" what she believed to be God's response. "What you do to the least of my brothers, you do for me. God is with you. Emmanuel."

"But how can we accomplish such a task?" Gail asked, the reality of what was ahead now becoming clear. "Can't you see? I don't know what I'm doing!"

"I will give you enough grace to meet each day's needs."

Gail felt weak, but she then sensed the Spirit of God slowly enveloping the entire room. Her eyes were still closed when she became aware of the presence of God in a way that she had never known before. She was afraid to open her eyes. The presence of God seemed so intense that she wondered if Jesus would be visible in that very room. Was she ready for this?

With what felt like electricity pouring through her body, Gail slowly lifted her head and opened her eyes. "I fully expected to have the child Jesus in my arms instead of Manuel," she said. God's presence was so overpowering that she began looking around the room, trying to find the real presence of Christ that was manifesting itself to her.

"My eyes stopped as I made the full circle," she said. "I gazed at Manuel, and I knew."

Gail relaxed, uttered a brief word of prayer, praise, and thanksgiving, and within minutes Manuel's seizures were over and Gail and Manuel were both fast asleep.

Gail and her husband are caring for a child that many people would say has no right to live. Manuel will never walk or talk. Though Gail displayed pictures to show that the three-and-a-half-year-old boy seems to recognize those around him, some doctors have disputed whether he can even know what's going on. But God knows, and Gail and her husband know, and Manuel is literally a conduit funneling a deeper sense of the presence of God into Gail's life.

> *We needn't limit our definition of caregiving to nursing sick people, however. The caregiver temperament incorporates many different avenues of loving God through serving others.*

We needn't limit our definition of caregiving to nursing sick people, however. The caregiver temperament incorporates many different avenues of loving God through serving others. Some might interpret giving care as quietly sitting by an elderly person's bed. Others might interpret it as working on a volunteer rescue unit or repairing a house. Activities to consider include:

"Adopting" a prisoner
Helping a friend through a personal crisis
Lending money
Helping somebody battling substance abuse
Volunteering on a rescue squad
Helping an illiterate person learn to read
Donating time at a battered women's shelter
Counseling at a pregnancy care center
Working in a soup kitchen
Fixing somebody's car
Repairing a house
Making recordings for the blind
Researching a cure for a disease

Helping somebody reconfigure their computer system

Watching the children of some tired parents

In his book *Conspiracy of Kindness* Steve Sjogren suggests mixing service with evangelism.[17] Imagine the surprise of neighbors if they see you providing soft drink giveaways in rush-hour traffic; providing hot chocolate, coffee, and cookies on a university campus; giving away free popsicles or cups of Gatorade to joggers, cyclists, or families at the local

> *Caring for others . . . provides evidence of a supernatural touch by God.*

park; raking leaves and mowing lawns in elderly communities; providing free kindling and firewood to the needy; and shoveling snow from sidewalks and driveways.

With the Spirit's inspiration guiding us, there is no limit to the number of opportunities available to those who seek to care for others. Whether we do this as a prelude to evangelism or as a service that demonstrates the love of Christ to others, it is a powerful picture of the gospel in action.

Caregivers as Prophets

Caring for others is a prophetic activity. Self-centered creatures that we are, being concerned about others is an unnatural response and provides evidence of a supernatural touch by God. In a very tangible way, then, the caregiver is a witness to God's existence by demonstrating his love through the giving of care.

According to the Bible, our natural human response is selfishness. The biblical pictures are plentiful: James and John wanting to sit at Jesus' right hand and the other disciples responding in resentment; Jacob plotting to get Esau's birthright; Lot taking the best piece of property; the priest and the Levite passing by the injured man as they traveled to Jericho.

We could add our own. I remember attending a meeting in high school of what was then called the "Key Club," which is a public service organization, and one of my friends commented, "Key Club is for people who have absolutely nothing to do with their time." Why should an active high school student care what happens in a nursing home, he thought.

Acts of selfishness can continue into marriage and career, as we just get too busy to care. I was greatly humbled one time when I was asked to speak at Swarthmore College for their "Why Jesus?" week of evangelism. When I got there, several students were meeting for prayer at 5:00 P.M. "Do you do this once a week?" I asked, impressed.

"No," they said. "Every day."

They don't have a campus pastor who watches over them. The school is considered too small by the national ministries. Instead, student leaders ask local pastors and Christian workers to come and speak at their weekly meetings.

One young woman shared during prayer requests about an investigative Bible study she had led the night before. Two other students shared about a two-hour follow-up session and a book table they'd be sitting at on campus the next day.

As I began mentally adding up the hours that these leaderless students were dedicating to God's work, I felt humbled and ashamed. There is so much free time in college, and physically, you really are at your prime. You can play football all day without feeling stiff for a week. You can go on lengthy hikes or to late-night movies without finding a baby-sitter. You can do all sorts of things, yet these students were dedicated to reaching the lost.

One young man was engaged to be married in the summer: "One hundred and sixteen days away," we were told.

"God," one collegian prayed, "help him to find one hundred and sixteen ways to serve you instead of just waiting for the wedding."

"Amen," the engaged man prayed.

These collegians were evidence of a supernatural touch that had lifted them out of their natural and sinful selfishness.

Yet rather than confront our selfishness, some Christian ministries may even try to exploit it. Instead of calling us to sacrifice out of love for Christ, one national relief agency ran an ad urging Christians to help them stop hunger because "It'll make you feel good." The message "You'll feel good about it" was repeated several times throughout the ad. As one writer observed, it is hard to imagine Christ saying, "Take up your cross and follow me; it'll make you feel good."[18]

Christians who demonstrate compassion because they are passionately in love with God will thus speak prophetically to a selfish culture and, sometimes, a selfish church. Selfishness distorts true sacrifice, and sacrifice is at the heart of true care. Mother Teresa of Calcutta said, "Real love is always painful and hurts: then it is real and pure."19 We have to pass through the pain of sacrifice before we experience the joy of obedience.

"Prophetic" caring, then, necessitates that we are caring out of love for God, that is, caring for others because we know God loves us so much. Wuthnow, a professor of sociology at Princeton University, writes that academic studies suggest the religious beliefs most conducive to care and compassion are a "personal God one can feel close to and a belief system that affirms one's personal worth." He goes on to write that "to the extent that one can measure such things in empirical studies, the perception that one is receiving love from God does in fact seem to be associated with a greater willingness to care for others."20

> *Christians who demonstrate compassion because they are passionately in love with God will thus speak prophetically to a selfish culture and, sometimes, a selfish church.*

The Temptations of Caregivers
Judging

When we are spiritually fed by showing care to others, we need to remember the lesson of Martha. We may think contemplatives are "too heavenly minded to be any earthly good" and prayer meetings are a waste of time if we're not making sure the Smiths, with a sick mother, are getting regular hot meals, but Jesus told Martha in very direct terms that there is a place for sitting at his feet in adoration.21

Caregiving is not a license to judge others who serve God in different ways. It is true that all Christians are called to care for others, but there are different ways this obligation can be fulfilled, and it is not for us to judge the validity of someone else's worship.

Serving Ourselves Through Serving Others

Some people with low self-worth may feel the need to serve others to validate their existence. Caregiving as a temperament means we express our love to God by reaching out to others; it's the picture of a heart overflowing with love and spilling out onto those around us. Caregiving as a disease is actually an act of taking; it's an act of deception, loving others so that they will love or need us in return.

One therapist said, "I really hate it when women get involved in volunteer organizations to take care of the great unwashed because they aren't taking care of business in their own lives. We do terrible things to people who already have enough problems without wanting them to also meet our needs."[22]

A Los Angeles priest gained national attention as "the minister of dollar handshakes." His idea of helping the poor was to cruise Skid Row every Sunday afternoon and pass out dollar bills to the homeless. One social worker wryly observed that this stroll "does nothing for the people but does a lot for Father Chase."[23]

Holding Narrow Definitions

Activists and caregivers may have more in common than you might think. Many caregivers may, in fact, be led to become activists. Someone who cares for the poor in the inner city may eventually be led to get involved in reforming government structures that get in the way.

It may be tempting, however, for a caregiver to judge the motives of an activist; but both can work together—one to help solve the underlying problem, the other to give comfort until the problem is addressed. Beware of narrowly defining care and thus missing the distinction between long-term, problem-solving care and short-term, problem-relieving care. Both have their place in kingdom work.

Neglecting Those Closest to Us

In our zeal to love God by loving others, we must remember that God makes home the priority. Paul writes to Timothy, "If anyone does not provide for his relatives, and especially for his immediate family, he has denied the faith and is worse than an unbeliever."[24] If we are truly loving God, and not just serving to satisfy our own needs, we will be content to care for those at home first. A young homemaker with small children can revolutionize her outlook if she sees that caring for her children is a major part of her worship. A young father must learn that changing the world begins in his own house.

Are You a Caregiver?

Are you a caregiver? Score the following statements on a scale of five to one, with five being very true and one being not true at all. Record your answer in the space provided.

_____ 1. I feel closest to God when I see him in the needy, the poor, the sick, and the imprisoned. I feel God's presence most strongly when I am sitting quietly beside the bed of someone who is lonely or ill or taking a meal to someone in need. You can count on me to offer a ride or volunteer for helping activities.

_____ 2. I grow weary of Christians who spend their time singing songs while a sick neighbor goes without a hot meal or a family in need doesn't get help fixing their car.

_____ 3. The words *service* and *compassion* are very appealing to me.

_____ 4. I sense God's power when I am counseling a friend who has lost a job, preparing meals for or fixing the car of a family in need, or spending a week at an orphanage in Mexico.

_____ 5. A book entitled *99 Ways to Help Your Neighbor* would be very appealing to me.

_____ 6. I would rather nurse someone to health or help someone repair their house than teach an adult Sunday school class, go on a prayer and fasting retreat, or take a lonely walk in the woods.

The total of all your answers. _____

Any score of fifteen or higher indicates a preference for this spiritual temperament. Take a moment now to register this score in chapter eleven on page 217 so you will have a composite picture of your soul's path to God.

The Call of Caregivers

It is one thing to say we believe; it's another to show compassion to others, to inconvenience ourselves because we believe. While such care is incumbent on every believer, some Christians will have a particular gift and calling for this type of service. These acts of mercy are a very practical way for them to show their love for God, but also to grow in their love for God. Caregivers may hear God more clearly when they change an adult's diaper than when they sit quietly in prayer.

> *It is one thing to say we believe; it's another to show compassion to others, to inconvenience ourselves because we believe.*

This is a high and holy calling. It won't be as visible as preaching to the crowds, but it is, I believe, particularly precious to our Father in heaven.

EIGHT

ENTHUSIASTS: LOVING GOD WITH MYSTERY AND CELEBRATION

There are worse places to die, I thought, looking up at the sun lighting the top of Crystal Mountain in Washington State. Some "friends" had offered to take me on what would be my first and last downhill skiing trip. I was old enough at the time to know that a body flying down a mountain past trees and boulders with two thin pieces of wood—neither of which has brakes—as your only contact with the ground, presented some dangers; possible death was the one that loomed foremost in my mind.

After I piddled around for a while, doing my best to ignore the five-year-olds who swept past me on what looked like rulers, my friends decided that the best way for me to learn was to go to the top of the mountain. If I could just get myself to the top, they figured, I'd have to come down.

I looked up Crystal Mountain and tried to decide which I preferred: slow and enduring humiliation in front of friends who would probably never forget my refusal, or a fairly quick death and dismemberment. I chose the latter.

The edge of the mountain looked like a snowy precipice leading to a frozen hell. I swallowed my fear and crammed a normally five-minute run into the next hour and a half. I told my friends that I wanted to make sure I didn't run into anybody; they were more worried about my back than what was in front of me, however. "Just stay out of the middle of the run," one warned.

"They're going a bit faster there, aren't they?" I said.

"Yeah, they're moving."

I could see that skiing had the potential to be an incredibly fun sport, but at that time I lacked the willingness to "let go" and send myself down the mountain. You can't ski very well if you need to check your speed every five yards. To get down the mountain before dinner, you've got to tuck the poles under your arms, point your skis downhill, and go for it—or so I'm told.

> *[Enthusiasts] like to let go and experience God on the precipice of excitement and awe.*

Downhill skiers remind me of enthusiast Christians. I was almost tempted to entitle this chapter "Loving God with Gusto." Enthusiasts enjoy a celebratory form of worship as well as many of the more supernatural forms of faith. People with this spiritual temperament like to let go and experience God on the precipice of excitement and awe.

This may make the enthusiast one of the more controversial of the spiritual temperaments. An honest look at Scripture, however, clearly reveals people of faith whose experiences involved generous portions of mystery, celebration, and supernatural events.

I understand the fear of many; supernatural experiences can all too easily degenerate into chaos. My response is to not deny this—it is all too true—but to suggest that this is precisely why the church must teach about legitimate and biblically ordained experiences of the supernatural. If the Christian church doesn't sanctify and oversee those practices taught and used by Christ and the apostles, then we are tempting people to experience these types of things outside the church where heresy is virtually certain. The best protection against New Age meditation, for instance, is biblically rooted Christian meditation. Some Christians may deny the heart's hunger for the transcendent, but they cannot still this desire. We can either teach people the way that God ordains for us to come into his presence, or leave them to stumble into it on their own. If these are the two choices, and I believe they are, then there is no question where I will end up—adopting the practices, but also the restraints, of the early apostles.

To begin to define the enthusiast temperament, I want to put two words into your mind—*mystery* and *celebration*. These two words help us to understand what feeds this type of Christian. We'll look at each element individually.

The Mystery of Faith

"Gary, how can I know God's will?"

"There are four ways we can discern God's will," I began, but internally I was thinking, *Now where did that come from?* Fortunately, four steps came to mind by the time I was done. I have spoken with dozens of teachers and counselors who have experienced the same thing.

"God," I prayed on another occasion, "this doesn't really square with what I think is the best way to discern your direction, but if you really do want me to begin this internship, I need to get these bills cleared up. Specifically, I need three hundred dollars by the end of the week."

The next day, I received a phone call from a close friend. "Gary," he said, "Jill and I have been praying. We think God wants us to give you a gift." The gift was a check for three hundred dollars.

Probably all of us, on either the receiving or giving end, have experienced something similar to these two situations. On one occasion we may be using a gift God has given us and say something that sounds profound and then think, "Where in the world did that come from?" Or a prayer is miraculously answered, in a way that makes coincidence seem impossible.

There is no getting around the fact that Christianity has its "mysterious" side. We worship and serve a supernatural God who manifests himself to us in supernatural ways. In this sense, every Christian will bear some marks of being an enthusiast. But enthusiasts *by temperament* are particularly fed by such experience. Enthusiasts long to preserve the mystery of faith. They understand that there are certain things about God and Christianity that we simply can't fully understand. When this understanding is rooted in anti-intellectualism, it becomes dangerous. When it is rooted in humility, in the understanding that God is spirit and we are flesh, that God is in control and we are not, it is a healthy response to a fantastic relationship between two unequals.

> There is no getting around the fact that Christianity has its "mysterious" side. We worship and serve a supernatural God who manifests himself to us in supernatural ways.

Accepting the mystery of faith has both its strengths and its dangers, for while there is much mystery and supernatural activity in Scripture, there are also strong warnings against improper manifestations of what is popularly called "spirituality." Before we get into the blessings of mystery, then, let's look at some of the warnings.

The Warnings

Many spiritual manifestations are expressly forbidden for the Christian. These include the list found in Deuteronomy 18:10–12: making children pass through fire, witchcraft, soothsaying, interpreting omens, sorcery, conjuring spells, acting as a medium or spiritist, and contacting the dead. Scripture is clear: "Anyone who does these things is detestable to the LORD." The pagan nations relied on these things, but the people belonging to YAHWEH were to rely on revelation from the Prophet,[1] ultimately Jesus Christ.[2]

A second warning can be inferred from knowing God as Creator. God gave us sound minds and solid, biblical revelation. These are in no sense inferior to "hearing God's voice." To suggest otherwise is to drive a wedge between God the Creator and God the Redeemer. We've probably all met Christians who had to "ask God" whether they should go out to eat or what street they should take to drive home:

"Want to go out for a burger?" we ask.

"Just a second," he says, and turns around, bowing his head. After a few moments of silence, he responds, "Nope, can't do it."

"Why not?"

"God told me not to."

Even more likely, we've met Christians (perhaps ourselves!) who have set up a "fleece"—à là Gideon—before taking a job or making a move. God's work with Gideon's fleece is clearly presented in Scripture as God making a concession rather than giving us a rule to practice. Still, for good or for bad, there seems to be something within us that needs more than mere reason to guide us.

How do we balance mystery and reason? King Saul's failure is a good lesson.

Saul got himself in great trouble when he disobeyed clear revelation and offered a sacrifice on his own because he felt "compelled" to do so.[3] God, who gave us our minds, doesn't despise us for using them, but he does get angry when we neglect them. God certainly doesn't expect us to accept without question any compulsion that comes our way, especially if we have written revelation to the contrary.

> God, who gave us our minds, doesn't despise us for using them, but he does get angry when we neglect them.

The Blessings

Apart from the warnings of Scripture, there are many ways "mystery" has become a part of faith. Three in particular are the use of dreams, expectancy, and prayer.

Dreams

One of the ways that God has moved, and continues to move, in mystery, is through dreams. In fact, most Christians with whom I have talked can point to one or two very significant dreams in their own lives.

One night a number of years ago, near the end of a vacation on the West Coast, I awoke from a particularly vivid dream. I dreamed that my boss at that time had resigned, and I saw his successor, a thin man with light hair. When I awoke, I prayed fervently and thought about it off and on until I told my wife about it the next morning.

After I got back to work I learned that on the same night of my dream, my boss had been asked to take on a different role in the organization and that a new president would be hired. He found this unacceptable and after many negotiations, eventually resigned. His successor was appointed several weeks later, a thin man with light hair.

Why did I have this dream? It served at least two purposes. First, it allowed me to intercede for a man I cared about in a moment of great distress for him. Second, it prepared me for major changes that were about to come into my life. I had more time to prepare for the ramifications, even though I had no "worldly" way of knowing what was happening.

I have talked with many other Christians who have heard from God in their sleep. A dream may have provided clear direction, a new insight into an ongoing struggle, or an encouragement or a rebuke, but I have talked with many whose faith has been strengthened by such experiences.

That God speaks through dreams is well established in Scripture. God spoke to Jacob, Joseph, Solomon, and Daniel through dreams.[4] Joel prophesied that when the Spirit of God would be poured out on believers, "your old men will dream dreams, your young men will see visions."[5]

The New Testament also contains accounts of God speaking to people through dreams, including Joseph and the three wise men.[6] There are also several visions, which differ from dreams in that the person receiving them is awake, in the New Testament. Paul, Ananias, Cornelius, and Peter all received visions.[7]

The idea of God speaking through a dream coincides with the nature of God. He is always pursuing us, speaking to us even while we sleep, giving evidence of his infinite and unlimited nature as opposed to our finite and limited existence. God has much to say to us, but we are often too busy to listen. Our minds have a tendency to get too occupied during the day, or sometimes we are too busy praying to God with our own agendas and have lost our listening ears. Dreams are one way God can "break in" and get something across to us that we might not be open to hearing during the day.

All of this must be put in context. I would never accept a dream that clashes with the revelation of Scripture. I would not make a major decision based solely on a dream. But I have found that God can bring insight into a situation, or give me warning, when I'm open to receiving something in a dream.

That God speaks through dreams is as strongly established in the history of the church as it is in Scripture. Augustine's mother had a dream in which her unruly son was converted to the faith, and this dream gave her the inspiration she needed to keep praying until Augustine turned to Christ. Such church luminaries as Justin Martyr, Irenaeus, Clement of Alexandria, Tertullian, Athanasius, Basil the Great, Gregory of Nazianzen, Gregory of Nyssa, John Chrysostom, Ambrose, Augustine, Jerome, and many others, accepted, to varying degrees, the idea of God speaking through select dreams.[8]

John Wesley wrote in his journal,

> What I have to say touching visions or dreams, is this: I know several persons in whom this great change was wrought in a dream, or during a strong representation to the eye of their mind, of Christ either on the cross or in glory. This is the fact; let any judge of it as they please.[9]

Twenty years later, Wesley acknowledged the fear many have of dreams, and he acknowledged that Satan can "mimic" legitimate dreams. Still, he believed dreams have a place.

> The danger was, to regard extraordinary circumstances too much.... Perhaps the danger is, to regard them too little; to condemn them altogether; to imagine they had nothing of God in them, and were a hindrance to his work. Whereas the truth is.... To strengthen and encourage them that believed, and to make his work more apparent, [God] favored several of them with divine dreams, others with trances and visions.[10]

As soon as we seek dreams for their own sake we have slipped from true Christianity to circus spirituality. On the other hand, it makes little sense to completely deny the usefulness of something just because it can be abused.

Let's look at some helps and safeguards related to our dreams.

The importance of listening. Many of us pay no attention to our dreams because we have ruled out the possibility that God could speak through them. And, in truth, the vast majority of our dreams are not messages from God—we'll talk more about this in a moment. Even so, the biblical and historical use of dreams is so prevalent that Christians should at least consider the possibility that God could speak to us in this way. If we're not listening, we may miss an important warning or word of instruction.

> *The biblical and historical use of dreams is so prevalent that Christians should at least consider the possibility that God could speak to us in this way.*

The importance of journaling. Most dreams will be lost within minutes if they are not written down. Journaling shows that we're serious about receiving God's direction, and it provides an opportunity for us to reflect and judge what we've heard. It will also help us to explain our dream to another and see if we are deceiving ourselves about its meaning.

The importance of meaning. The dreams in which God was clearly speaking in my life have been very clear in their "interpretation." If God is speaking, I don't have to figure the dreams out. I wake up with the understanding. This is an important point with biblical precedent. In the Bible, members outside of the community of faith, such as Pharaoh and Nebuchadnezzar, required a member of the community of faith to interpret their dreams (Joseph and Daniel, respectively).[11] But people belonging to God, such as Joseph and Paul, seemed to have the interpretation clear in their minds as soon as they awoke.[12]

Thus, we should draw a distinction between schools of thought that "interpret" dreams through psychoanalysis and symbol, and a biblical understanding of receiving both the dream and the meaning upon waking. If the interpretation isn't clear upon waking, hold any insight loosely, and wait for additional confirmation.

The importance of community. Any attempt to grow in this area of Christian spirituality apart from the body of Christ is outright dangerous. Without the firm foundation of biblical truth for our absolute standard, the wisdom of Christian tradition and history for our general guidance, and the contemporary oversight of fellow believers for accountability, we can easily be led astray. If you're not connected to a local church, your first step toward spiritual growth should be to find one.

The importance of perspective. When you begin accepting the possibility of God speaking through a dream, you may find yourself remembering far more of your dreams than you did before. In fact, just the process of reviewing your dreams upon waking will begin making you more aware of them after just a few days. However, because we dream every night, the practice of listening through our dreams can become very dangerous. Here's why.

Tertullian believed that dreams come from three sources: the natural workings of our soul, demons, or God.[13] The natural workings of our soul probably count for ninety-eight percent or more of our dreams, and the latter two categories make up the remaining two percent. If we adopt Tertullian's view of the three sources of dreams, we find that two out of the three can lead us astray. If the dream is the natural working out of our soul's fears, nightmares, and anxieties, we certainly don't want to guide our lives by these fears and anxieties. Even our soul's hopes can lead us astray if our personal dreams conflict with God's will for us.

And because, at least according to Tertullian, Satan can use our dreams to masquerade as an angel of light, we must be especially careful about what we accept. I read one account of a woman who had her dream examined by a Christian counselor, and the alleged leading of the dream was that she should move forward in seeking a divorce. It is precisely this type of occurrence that makes me so nervous about "interpreting" dreams. Not only are the sources of dreams suspect, but our interpretations are suspect as well. Scripture is very clear that legitimate grounds for divorce are very narrowly defined, and certainly a dream should never be used to counteract the clear teaching of Scripture.

God clearly uses dreams in Scripture, and I've found in my own life and the experiences of others that God can continue, on a limited basis, to use them today; but we must avoid reducing our faith to waking up every morning and thinking, *Now, what was God telling me last night?* This is a clear abuse of a practice that God infrequently uses to guide his people. If we want to hear from God, the first place to go is Scripture.

Dreams can also point us to another aspect of living out our "mysterious" faith, the importance of expectancy.

Expectancy

While a young collegian, I met with a number of students every Friday afternoon on the top floor of a dorm for prayer. We called these meetings the "Upper Room." They were powerful times of preparation for our Friday night campus meetings.

> *Enthusiasts "need" this expectancy in their faith. A planned program in which God is not invited to move—even if he should be inclined to do so—would seem unbearably stifling.*

One of the things that charged these lengthy prayer times was expectancy. We expected that God wanted to do something, and he often met that expectancy and then some. The theme of our prayers often became or coincided with the theme of the Friday night meetings, even when those planning the meetings had no idea what we were praying about across campus. This happened so frequently that my future wife, then girlfriend, frequently asked me as we walked in to the meeting, "So what are we going to hear about tonight?"

Enthusiasts "need" this expectancy in their faith. A planned program in which God is not invited to move—even if he should be inclined to do so—would seem unbearably stifling.

The problem is that the church as an institution needs some boundaries. If everybody who felt God moving through them blurted out a pronouncement or word of instruction, the church service would soon resemble a carnival. Paul dealt with this at some length in his correspondence with the Corinthians. That's why I usually encourage enthusiasts to incorporate expectancy into their personal life, the Monday through Saturday side of their walk with God.

To cultivate the mystery of expectancy, enthusiasts would do well to wake up and ask God to bring someone in their path to whom they can minister. This sense of watching, whether it presents an evangelistic opportunity or a chance to encourage a downhearted believer, energizes enthusiasts' faith because they see God moving in visible ways.

The needs out in the "real world" are great and known to God. By cooperating with him we can move in supernatural ways. The reality of this came home to me in a new way when I was walking through the mall helping a friend pick out a tiny bear to place in the coffin of his stillborn son. We were ripped up inside, trying to carry on a normal conversation with various store clerks, while emotionally we were bruised and battered and feeling like crying.

It hit me that virtually every time I step inside a mall, the odds are that somebody feels just like my friend and I did that day. Maybe they just found out they have cancer or that a close loved one has cancer; maybe they're going through a divorce or their parents are going through a divorce. A spouse may have just been laid off or fired, while another may suspect an affair. Any number of deeply felt crises are going on in people's lives, but in our busyness, our lack of expectancy, we miss opportunities to minister to people in supernatural ways.

Spiritual risk-taking is another way to foster this expectancy. Beginning a conversation with a stranger in hopes of sharing the gospel or stepping out in faith in an unknown situation can charge an enthusiast's faith. We don't want to slip into the sin of presumption here, as if God is obligated to provide such excitement on a daily or even monthly basis. On the other hand, complacency and being lukewarm is no less a sin than presumption.

Be willing to stretch yourself. Don't run from situations in which the natural obstacles appear insurmountable. Create room in your life for God to move. If finances are tight and you need to make a major purchase, give God the chance to provide first. If finances are plentiful, be open to clues about how you can meet another's need.

Prayer

Is there anything more mysterious than prayer? Prayer moves us to call upon a Being we cannot see and ask him to alter that which we can see. Enthusiasts need to create pockets of prayer in their lives, learning to trust God to come through in unexpected ways.

However, there is an element of mystery against which many enthusiasts sometimes rebel, and that is the mystery of unanswered prayer, or, perhaps more appropriately stated, prayers that are answered "no." Because God sometimes answers our prayers with a "yes," it can become intoxicating, especially to the enthusiast, and that intoxication can become so addicting that we begin to demand that God answer every prayer with a "yes." When a prayer isn't answered in the way we want it to be answered, we may mistakenly assume there must be hidden sin, lack of faith, or some other minute item that sends us into hours of fruitless introspection.

It's been said before, but is worth repeating here: To demand that God answer all our prayers with a "yes" is to ask for his omnipotence (power) without having the benefit of his omniscience (knowledge).

To demand that God answer all our prayers with a "yes" is to ask for his omnipotence (power) without having the benefit of his omniscience (knowledge).

Looking back, I'm thankful God said "no" to some of my prayers. The mystery of faith calls us to love and serve a God whom we can't always understand. The enthusiast loves this when the result is satisfying, and God answers in ways that make our knees weak. It is much less exciting, however, when the mystery leads us to believe that God is silent, indifferent, or even cruel. Mystery is mystery. It has its exhilarating elements as well as its frustrating elements. We can't expect one without the other.

The necessity of maturity will probably lead virtually every enthusiast through this canyon of unanswered prayer, where expectancy runs dry and the only mystery seems to be where God is hiding. Understand that this is a necessary avenue on the destination to holiness and that it usually has an end—in God's timing, however.

Acts of Celebration

In addition to mystery, the enthusiast is fed through celebration. Let's look at some of the ways celebration can be incorporated and fostered in our faith and worship.

I'll always remember the morning I finished my first, full-length, published book. I had been writing for a good nine years, preparing for that day. At one point, I had received over one hundred and fifty straight rejections of various articles and proposals. After numerous false starts and completed books that never made it out of my drawer, I was making the final touches to a manuscript that was under contract.

It was early in the morning and nobody else was in the office. I marveled at what God had given me: the strength to persevere, insights that went beyond my natural ability, open doors with a publisher. Once the package was bundled up and ready to go, I spent time celebrating before God in a way that I hadn't done for years. I remembered the morning, several years before, when I had woken up and felt God urging me, "Write, write, write," and I complained, "What for? Nobody's reading it!"

> *In the midst of a celebration it's easy to forget how fearful and awesome God is. Without reverence, however, celebration degenerates into shallow triviality.*

But now God had broken through. I was familiar with the call to sacrifice hours of leisure, to persevere past doubt, to die to my desire to sleep in—but now came the fun part.

Now it was time to party.

Those that know me know that the call to celebrate can be more difficult for me to obey than the call to sacrifice. I'm not a natural celebrator. I probably emphasize the call of the gospel on our lives more than its benefits. That's just my nature. But I'm trying to learn from the enthusiast. I'm trying to understand how to participate in the joyful recognition that we serve an absolutely wonderful God and have so much about which to celebrate.

Celebration can take many different forms and could be a book in itself, so we'll confine ourselves to just a few choice examples, including enthusiastic worship, spending time with children, and being involved in creative endeavors.

Enthusiastic Worship

Celebration has a wide background in Scripture. There were at least three major feasts prescribed in the Old Testament—Passover, Pentecost, and Tabernacles—and several other religious celebrations. These could be elaborate affairs. The Feast of Tabernacles, for example, involved a seven-day feast in which the Israelites are commanded to rejoice.[14]

Programmed celebration also gave way to individual, spontaneous celebration. David, the man after God's own heart, danced enthusiastically before the ark of the covenant, and when his wife despised him for it, he replied that the Lord had chosen him, and in response he would celebrate and "become even more undignified than this."[15]

David also appointed singers and musicians, that they might worship and "sing joyful songs."[16] A musical, celebratory style of worship was one of the hallmarks of David's era: "David and all the Israelites were celebrating with all their might before God, with songs and with harps, lyres, tambourines, cymbals and trumpets."[17] Many years later, Israel was still using the instruments commissioned by David.[18]

Jesus also encouraged celebratory styles of worship. Not only did he and his disciples participate in hymn-singing,[19] but when religious leaders complained about the people's loud celebration of Christ's entrance into Jerusalem, Jesus said, "I tell you, if [the people] keep quiet, the stones will cry out."[20]

This celebratory style is carried over into apostolic, New Testament worship as well. Acts 2 foretells speaking in tongues, receiving dreams, witnessing signs, and experiencing wonders. Paul and Silas sing hymns while in prison, and Paul exhorts the Ephesians to use psalms, hymns, and spiritual songs in their worship.[21]

According to the book of Revelation, worship in heaven involves crying out "in a loud voice," and the roar of a great multitude shouting "Hallelujah!"[22]

All of this tells me that my reluctance to celebrate enthusiastically is more a personal foible than a sign of maturity. It's something I need to overcome instead of something to be proud of. When Jesus says, "I tell you, if the people keep silent, the stones will cry out," I'm convicted. We have even more reason to celebrate the risen Christ today than when Jesus entered Jerusalem before the Crucifixion.

There are some warnings given to celebrants, however. While the apostles participated in supernatural activities, they still found it necessary to include formal and structured religious observances in their worship.[23] Paul stressed that order was extremely important,[24] and Revelation 19:20 tells us that miracles and signs can deceive as well as inspire. Furthermore, Simon is chastised for seeking a supernatural gift rather than the Giver.[25]

It's also important to point out that celebratory worship must still include reverence. In the midst of a celebration in which the ark of the covenant was brought back to Israel, those carrying the ark must surely have had light hearts even while carrying a heavy load. Festive music—with tambourines, harps, cymbals, and trumpets—filled the air. David and the Israelites celebrated "with all their might." In the middle of this joyous celebration, the ark rocked slightly and Uzza, forgetting what he was carrying, reached out to touch the ark. Immediately Uzza died.[26]

> *In the midst of a celebration it's easy to forget how fearful and awesome God is. Without reverence, however, celebration degenerates into shallow triviality.*

In the midst of a celebration it's easy to forget how fearful and awesome God is. Without reverence, however, celebration degenerates into shallow triviality. It's interesting to note that in a later psalm, recorded in 1 Chronicles 16—after Uzza's death—David includes both celebration and reverence: "Sing to him, sing praise to him. . . . Tremble before him, all the earth!"[27] David had learned his lesson: celebration must never lose touch with what Isaac called the "Fear" of Israel.

The act of celebration reminds us that we have much to be thankful for. God is worthy of great praise, and who else will sing that praise if not those who believe? There was a fifth-century group of Greek monks who were known as the "non-sleepers" because they frequently spent an entire day and night in uninterrupted praise of God. Most of us may not have the strength to do that, but let us remember that God is worthy of even more than that. Even our best (though acceptable to him) will always be far less than God deserves. But even more than an obligation, celebration is a privilege. Celebrative worship leads to joy, which is a foundational virtue leading to spiritual strength.[28]

Spending Time with Children

For those Christians who have lost the ability or inclination to celebrate, spending time with children might be a good way to recapture the joy and wonder of our faith.

I was driving along a boring highway listening to mindless chatter on the radio when God broke into my thoughts through the voice of my then five-year-old daughter. It was near Christmastime, and I listened as Allison spoke: "Isn't it amazing, Daddy, that God became a little baby?"

Allison's wonder and delight polished a too familiar truth and brought back its shining beauty. She infused my Christmas with her own wonder and amazement; it was absolutely the best Christmas present anyone ever gave me.

Jesus said, "Unless you change and become like little children, you will never enter the kingdom of heaven." He also said, "Let the little children come to me, and do not hinder them, for the kingdom of heaven belongs to such as these."[29] Enthusiasts can treat these passages literally and learn all about loving God by watching children. In this sense, volunteering in the church nursery is much more than service; it is a worship experience in itself.

The burdens, demands, and obligations of life can stifle adult fellowship. Sometimes adult banter is nothing less than depressing. Spending time with children is a good way to gain a new perspective and to remember a time when life still held hope, promise, and joy.

If your children are grown, pull out some old picture albums and marvel at what God has done through the years. Let the reality of a baby grown into a mature woman or man call you back to the essence of life, to things eternal.

Creating

One of the more difficult things I've been called on to do was to officiate at a funeral service for a young man who died of AIDS. He never married, didn't father any children, and because he had built a list of legal offenses and arrests long enough to fill a computer screen, he ultimately died in prison. The last few years of his life were a torturous affair; he never could learn to live without heroin (which is how the HIV virus was introduced to his body).

> Whether it's building a business, writing a poem, painting a picture, or planting a garden, creating something can be a profoundly holy experience.

This young man had great promise—but died with most of that promise unfulfilled. Christians rightly believe that life is a gift given to us by God—something we shouldn't waste. We celebrate God by using the life he has given us to create other things. Whether it's building a business, writing a poem, painting a picture, or planting a garden, creating something can be a profoundly holy experience. Far more than hobbies, these activities can be powerful expressions of worship. One of the most powerful antidotes to addiction is participating in different activities, lifting the addicts out of themselves and into positive, constructive acts of creation.

Healthy Christians create. It is the nature of our God to create. He's introduced in Genesis 1 as the Creator of everything. One of the last images given to us in the book of Revelation is God creating the new heaven and the new earth. The Bible is literally framed around the act of God creating.

With the Spirit of God living in us we, too, need to create. I won't create the same things that my wife or children create, but all of us should find some participation in the act of creation. It's what we were made to do.

When looking at creating as an act of worship, it is preferable to choose something you're relatively good at, or at least inclined toward; frustration is a pretty effective block to adoration. Without lapsing into perfectionism, do your best to make something shine for the glory of God. God gave you your mind, your hands, your strength, and your skill—make something to give that mind, strength, and skill back to God.

Think carefully about how you can cooperate with God to bring forth something new—how that landscape can be restored; how a new program of education might restore lives and hope to young people; how a sculpture could reflect on the beauty of a heavenly theme; how even a cosmetic surgeon can create a new life for a child with a grotesque deformity.

Enthusiasts and Bible Reading

The elements of mystery and celebration that we've discussed can affect how we read Scripture. While a good solid study program is a must for every believer, enthusiasts can "spice up" their Bible reading by incorporating mystery and celebration. Let's spend just a few brief moments discussing how enthusiasts can "recharge" their daily Bible study.

Enthusiasts must take care to remain rooted in good, solid biblical training. The good news is that, according to Evelyn Underhill, there are three faculties of the worshiping spirit, and the enthusiast excels in two out of the three: feeling, imagination, and the reasoning mind. The first two, feeling and imagination, can help enthusiasts build up the third area, a reasoning mind.[30]

In this form of Bible study, the Christian uses both feeling and reason to ponder a scene from Scripture or one of the truths presented by Scripture. Imagination can be used to place oneself at the scene, watching Jesus call the children to gather around him, for instance, and imagining what it must have been like to be one of the children or perhaps one of their parents.

Imagination can also be used to consider how the teaching of Scripture can be actualized in our lives. When Scripture calls us to be gentle, we imagine responding in a gentle manner to our children, spouse, or coworkers. If Scripture is calling us to a particularly difficult encounter—asking forgiveness or confessing a sin, for example—we can prayerfully imagine the fulfillment of that encounter with Christ nearby, comforting us, giving us the courage to confront the situation in real life.

The use of imagination and feeling can give "legs" to the teaching we've received, helping us to hang on to it longer. It can also help the enthusiast study the Bible in a format particularly suited to his or her temperament.

Seeking miraculous experiences simply for the sake of experiencing the miraculous makes us spiritual drug addicts who simply want to get "high."

Saint John Eudes taught his disciples to study the Gospels by first reconstructing the event (imagination); discerning the meaning (mind); responding with the appropriate emotion—be it adoration, penitence, or something else (heart); and concluding with a firm commitment (will).[31] This is a full and comprehensive approach to Bible study that uses all our faculties.

The Temptations of Enthusiasts

While the enthusiast temperament points to many exciting strengths, there are also some inherent weaknesses that enthusiasts need to be warned about.

Seeking Experiences for Experiences' Sake

Seeking miraculous experiences simply for the sake of experiencing the miraculous makes us spiritual drug addicts who simply want to get "high." This book is about learning to love God, not learning to join a spiritual circus.

Enthusiasts need to be especially careful to remain true to seeking and loving God rather than searching for new experiences. When we seek "spiritual experiences" for their own sake, they can actually become, and be used for, evil.

Being Independent

Enthusiasts, perhaps more than any other temperament, need to be rooted in a strong church that can hold individual believers accountable. Supernatural experience apart from the oversight of the church is a sure prescription for disaster. Kelsey writes, "The idea that each person's religious opinion is of the same value is nonsense, for there is a body of knowledge which is tested by time that can be transmitted by the church to believers."[32]

Scripture may be our final authority, but it is foolish to ignore the wisdom learned from believers in the past and applied by believers in the present. The apostle Paul, who experienced spiritual reality that most of us could only dream about, made sure he submitted himself to the counsel of the apostles in Jerusalem.

Equating "Good Feelings" with "Good Worship"

Pure worship is an act of our will in which we offer our allegiance, praise, and thanksgiving to God. Just because we feel good during a time of worship doesn't mean we have offered up our will in an appropriate manner. Conversely, just because we feel down or "flat" doesn't mean we aren't effectively worshiping God.

Feelings come and go. Enthusiasts shouldn't apologize for enjoying them, but they should avoid becoming dependent upon them.

Are You an Enthusiast?

Are you an enthusiast? Score the following statements on a scale of five to one, with five being very true and one being not true at all. Record your answer in the space provided.

_____ 1. I feel closest to God when my heart is sent soaring and I feel like I want to burst, worship God all day long, and shout out his Name. Celebrating God and his love is my favorite form of worship.

_____ 2. God is an exciting God, and we should be excited about worshiping him. I don't understand how some Christians can say they love God, and then act like they're going to a funeral whenever they walk into church.

_____ 3. The words *celebration* and *joy* are very appealing to me.

_____ 4. I would enjoy attending a workshop on learning to worship through dance or attending several worship sessions with contemporary music. I expect that God is going to move in some unexpected ways.

_____ 5. I would enjoy reading the book *The Mystery and Excitement of Walking with God*.

_____ 6. I spend more money on music and worship tapes than on books.

The total of all your answers. _____

Any score of fifteen or higher indicates a preference for this spiritual temperament. Please take a moment to register this score in chapter eleven on page 217 so you will have a composite picture of your soul's path to God.

The Message of Enthusiasts

Sometimes life can squeeze joy out of us faster than it can be replenished. I was talking with a friend once who had undergone some real financial difficulties. After a long struggle, he began making progress. Just when he began to have new hope, however, the company he worked for received a review from a consultant, terminated his position, and offered him another position with considerably lower pay.

It is difficult—and can even seem inappropriate—to remain positive and enthusiastic in the face of such changes. Because of this, the enthusiast temperament is often seen as obnoxious, naive, or immature. "Just wait until their eyes are opened," some cynics might say. "They won't be quite so upbeat then."

Early in my writing career I remember talking to a published author about a book idea. He gave me all the "doom and gloom" about publishing and basically told me I was wasting my time. A pastor overheard our conversation. I didn't know him, but I'll always remember his words: "Don't give up. If God is calling you to do this, it'll happen."

For me, that pastor was the voice of the enthusiast. In a cynical and depressed world, enthusiasts point toward faith, mystery, and expectancy. When the situation seems impossible, enthusiasts say, "Now God's *really* going to move." God doesn't always move the way we hope he will or the way we want him to, but despair and cynicism cloud real faith as much as Pollyanna optimism clouds real life.

> *In a cynical and depressed world, enthusiasts point toward faith, mystery, and expectancy.*

Sometimes God does move in strange and powerful ways. People are miraculously healed; lives are dramatically turned around; hearts are at once challenged, convicted, and encouraged through a supernatural event.

A friend of mine was weeping at the altar of a conference, knowing that God was calling her to release her fears for her children and hand them over to him. As she sat there praying, an anxious pastor, who had absolutely no earthly way of knowing what was going on, walked up and said, "I'm really nervous about saying this, but I believe God wants you to hear this Scripture."

The pastor turned to the passage where Hannah gives up Samuel. My friend was overwhelmed, knowing God had read her heart and was giving her direction.

I know, *I know*, for every powerful story like this one there are at least a dozen instances where people really miss the mark and say something stupid. But none of this denies the fact that Scripture and church history are full of accounts where God moves mysteriously and powerfully, sometimes confronting entire nations, at other times reaching just one individual. And my friend was profoundly encouraged by that timely passage.

Personally, I don't score very high as an enthusiast. I prefer meditative walks in the woods to loud celebrations. I'd rather grapple with the truth of a scriptural passage than listen to a dream. But I have to admit, I don't celebrate God one-tenth as much as he deserves to be celebrated. And I have a sinful tendency to lapse into a practical "atheism," believing in God, but not expecting him to move in supernatural ways.

I believe enthusiasts have a precious gift and a special calling, and I hope that they will never stop celebrating and never stop believing, even in the darkest night.

NINE

CONTEMPLATIVES: LOVING GOD THROUGH ADORATION

Larry Crabb, a best-selling author and Christian counselor, has probably had thousands of social lunches and dinners in his lifetime, but one will always stand out in his mind. While speaking at a spiritual journey conference at Biola University (in California), Larry shared a meal with Dr. James Houston, a professor from Regent College (Vancouver, B.C.). In Larry's words, "When I was with him . . . I experienced something coming out of him that touched a part of my soul that isn't often touched. . . . I went to my bedroom and I literally wept. I fell on my knees and I said, 'Lord, I'll pay any price to know who you are.'"

When I read of this encounter in a Regent College publication, I smiled knowingly. I had a similar experience sitting in Dr. Houston's classes when I attended Regent College. There is something about men and women who have devoted themselves to knowing God that touches our souls in a profound way.

By build, by speech, and by character, Dr. Houston has all the marks of an English gentleman. When Regent was being shaped out of two old fraternity houses, Dr. Houston stripped old wallpaper while wearing shirtsleeves and a tie. When you look at him, there is nothing "mystical" or effeminate about him in any way, yet I remember sitting fascinated as this man spoke candidly and openly about "holding hands with God."

Holding hands with God?

"As two lovers do nothing but gaze into each other's eyes, so we gaze lovingly at our heavenly Father and have our heart's delight satisfied."

I listened to these words before Dr. Houston had introduced me to Teresa of Avila. My prayer life at that time consisted of an ever-lengthening intercession list. I had divided it into different days to give me plenty of time to "wrestle" in prayer. But the type of prayer Dr. Houston was talking about had nothing at all to do with wrestling. He was talking about holding hands and building, in his words, a "transforming friendship." This was one of my first introductions to the way of the contemplative.

The contemplative seeks to perform the first work of adoring God. God is known and described as the heavenly spouse in whom all the contemplative's delight is met. While some seek to serve the Lord, others seek to celebrate him, and still others seek to explain him, the contemplative seeks to gaze lovingly into God's face and be caught up in the rapture of a lover's experience.

The Biblical Portrayal of Contemplatives

Contemplatives remind us that God does not seek obedient but dispassionate servants, but rather a passionate love that is so strong it burns all other bonds.

One of the best descriptions of the role of contemplatives is found in Moses' prophecy/description of the tribe of Benjamin: "Let the beloved of the LORD rest secure in him, for he shields him all day long, and the one the LORD loves rests between his shoulders."[1]

"Resting between God's shoulders" is the favorite pastime of contemplatives. They want to enjoy God and learn to love him in ever deeper ways. Contemplatives remind us that God does not seek obedient but dispassionate servants, but rather a passionate love that is so strong it burns all other bonds. Even the Old Testament describes a love relationship between God and his chosen people.

> The LORD did not set his affection on you and choose you because you were more numerous than other peoples, for you were the fewest of all peoples. But it was because the LORD loved you and kept the oath he swore to your forefathers that he brought you out with a mighty hand and redeemed you from the land of slavery.[2]

Listen particularly to key passages in David's Psalm 63.

> O God, you are my God,
> earnestly I seek you;
> my soul thirsts for you,
> my body longs for you,
> in a dry and weary land
> where there is no water. . . .
> Because your love is
> better than life,
> my lips will glorify you. . . .
> My soul will be satisfied as with
> the richest of foods;
> with singing lips my mouth will praise you. . . .
> I think of you through the watches of the night. . . .
> My soul clings to you.[3]

The Song of Songs, though clearly legitimizing deep and passionate love between a husband and wife, has often been traditionally understood as a picture of the love relationship between God and his people. Passages like the following speak of this abiding, "hand-holding" love.

The Shulamite woman proclaims, "He has taken me to the banquet hall, and his banner over me is love. Strengthen me with raisins, refresh me with apples, for I am faint with love."[4]

This passionate yearning leads to a vigorous search: "All night long on my bed I looked for the one my heart loves; I looked for him but did not find him. I will get up now and go about the city, through its streets and squares; I will search for the one my heart loves." When the lover is found, the Shulamite sings, "When I found the one my heart loves . . . I held him and would not let him go."[5]

These frank and unashamed words should not surprise us in light of the charge given to the community of faith in Deuteronomy 6:5: "Love the LORD your God with all your heart and with all your soul and with all your strength." Cold and calculated lip service is not enough for our God. "The LORD says: 'These people come near to me with their mouth and honor me with their lips, but their hearts are far from me.'"[6]

God's love for his people is so intense that when Israel strays from God, the act is often analogized as the betrayal of adultery. In Jeremiah, God remembers fondly the love relationship he had with Israel. "I remember the devotion of your youth, how as a bride you loved me and followed me through the desert."[7] God feels our rejection so strongly that his pain at our straying is no less than a husband who finds out his wife has been unfaithful. We may think, "God doesn't need me!" On a practical matter, he doesn't need to need us, but he chooses to need us in the sense that he feels our rejection or passionate return deeply.

There was a time in my life when I thought Christianity was about being obedient, and the ultimate issue was whether I would end up in heaven or hell. As I matured, I found that Christianity was about intimacy with the Father, and obedience was one of the necessary roads I travel as I lovingly relate to God. I started relating to heaven and hell less as places and more as descriptions of communion or separation from God. (I'm speaking figuratively, of course. Both heaven and hell have a literal separate existence apart from this sense of relationship.)

Unfortunately, throughout the history of faith, some well-meaning men and women have failed to grasp the depth and calling of this love relationship with God, preferring instead to turn faith into ethical lists of dos and don'ts. This rote obedience apart from adoration is not the faith that Jesus represented. When a woman extravagantly pours expensive perfume on Christ's head, some of the disciples vehemently object, but Jesus defends her act as an acceptable offering of love, acceptable even above giving to the poor. The act is so full of adoration and love and so acceptable in Jesus'

> *It is not unusual for contemplatives to be misunderstood and judged by others.*

sight that Jesus promises, "Wherever this gospel is preached throughout the world, what she has done will also be told, in memory of her."[8]

It is not unusual for contemplatives to be misunderstood and judged by others. Martha, busy in her service to Jesus, found herself rebuked, not for performing her service, but for judging Mary, a contemplative.[9] Jesus was not about to distract Mary from her calling to gaze lovingly on the face of her Lord.

The activist may have a hard time accepting the contemplative. The traditionalist might think the contemplative shallow. The intellectual might find the contemplative's worship to be nothing less than a mystery. The enthusiast might find the contemplative's worship to be boring. But to God the contemplative's worship is cherished, valued, and rewarded.

God's Beloved

A quick look at the historical role of contemplatives will help us to better understand this spiritual temperament. Historically, a distinction has been drawn between "active meditation" and "infused contemplation." In active meditation, Christians vigorously seek God; infused contemplation is more something that is done *to* Christians; it leaves them passive in what is virtually a sense-less experience, variously described as the dark night of faith or the "cloud of unknowing."

We don't have the space to get into the intricacies of such distinctions here, but it is important to remember that *every* true Christian experience is, in one sense, "infused." We are called to cooperate with God, but even our willingness to cooperate, and certainly the strength to cooperate, is a gift from God. Mature contemplation, then, is a work of the Holy Spirit. God must infuse us with love in order for us to love.

We can become active and cooperative agents, however, by emptying our lives of those things that choke out our desire for God. I wrote at some length about "cultivating the quiet" and the Christian discipline of submission in *Seeking the Face of God*;[10] so here let us be reminded by another writer, Thomas Merton, who wrote: "The fact remains that contemplation will not be given to those who willfully remain at a distance from God, who confine their interior life to a few routine exercises of piety and a few external acts of worship and service performed as a matter of duty. . . . God does not manifest Himself to these souls because they do not seek Him with any real desire."[11]

While I explained earlier that my discipline of an hour-long, daily quiet time had to be altered somewhat, I've found that some sort of quiet time is still essential, if for no other reason than to set my desire on serving and pleasing God the rest of the day. Morning is the crucial time to do this because it colors the rest of my day with what Merton calls "real desire."

> *Christian contemplation has less to do with mystical experience than it has to do with adoration. Jesus was emphatic that the spiritual life is based on love, not laws.*

Thomas Aquinas explains that contemplation will be denied to a man in proportion to how much he belongs to the world. We can't make ourselves love God, but we can prepare the way and, according to Aquinas, desire is the most important thing in the contemplative life.[12]

In the study of Christian spirituality, real contemplation is actually an experience with a beginning and an end that Christians pass through. Contemplation is not generally considered a life-state that one exists in, so I'm adapting the word somewhat when I use it as a label for a spiritual temperament.

Here is how one writer explains Augustine's description of this experience:

The act of contemplation is [characterized by Augustine] as "the perception of Something Unchangeable," accompanied by a wondrous inward joy. Its effect on the soul is to make it feel contempt for exterior things, and be ravished by things interior. But after the brief moment of realization, the soul, weighed down by the burden of its infirmity, sinks back to its ordinary level and its normal experience: and this return, as it were, from the other world is an occasion of sorrow, and of longing for a renewal of the experience. Here is emphasized what is the testimony of all the mystics as to the transient nature of the act of contemplation.[13]

I was tempted to name this temperament "Beloved" because Christian contemplation has less to do with mystical experience than it has to do with adoration. Jesus was emphatic that the spiritual life is based on love, not laws. The greatest commandment, he said, is to love the Lord our God with all our heart, soul, mind, and strength. Jesus told his disciples, "I no longer call you servants, . . . I have called you friends."[14]

Servants is a "doing" word; *friends* is a "being" word. What do servants do? They cook, clean, et cetera. A friend, however, is something you are, not something you do. A servant is Martha, a friend is Mary.

For our purposes, I will describe contemplation as a form of "hand-holding prayer" in which the Christian rests in God's presence. Thomas Merton writes that "there are so many Christians who have practically no idea of the immense love of God for them, and of the power of that Love to do them good, to bring them happiness."[15] But contemplatives live for this love. They want nothing more than some privacy and quiet to gaze upon the face of their heavenly lover and give all of themselves to God.

> *Contemplatives simply want to bathe in the ocean of love God has for his children, while the rest of us seem unfortunately content to experience that love drop by drop.*

It is impossible to understand the contemplative apart from this motivation of love. Many people think of "mystics" as loners, or even, in an ascetic setting, masochists. But really, contemplatives simply want to bathe in the ocean of love God has for his children, while the rest of us seem unfortunately content to experience that love drop by drop.

Are you catching the love relationship that fuels contemplatives? Without hesitancy, with no sense of obligation, contemplatives appreciate Christ with unadulterated adoration. Time is one of the best gifts we can give God, and contemplatives want to give God plenty.

It's important to mention another distinction that is crucial to the worship of contemplatives. Contemplatives seek the perception of God's being or presence, but this is something different from a divine vision of God's essence. It may be that both Paul and Moses were blessed with such experiences, but these are truly unusual, thoroughly miraculous occurrences, and undoubtedly very rare. When I talk about seeking God's face, then, I am not generally talking about actually seeing God's face as much as I am talking about being aware of his presence.

Acts of Contemplatives

There are many forms of prayer and activity that contemplatives can make use of in addition to general contemplative prayer. Let's look at a few of them.

The Jesus Prayer

Historically, contemplatives have made great use of the "Jesus Prayer," a very simple prayer that runs like this: "Lord Jesus Christ, son of God, have mercy on me, a sinner." Sometimes an even shorter form might be used. Cassian, a famous fifth-century monk, used the prayer, "Come to my aid, God; Lord, make haste to help me."[16]

The purpose of the Jesus prayer is to practice the presence of God, and its usefulness has been proven through the ages. It has also occasionally been abused to become an end in itself. One monk, for instance, started out by saying it 10,000 times a day, eventually working up to over 100,000 times a day. This is just evidence that a good practice can be pushed into absurdity. If we're so caught up with how many times we're saying something, we're no longer focusing on why we're saying it. (Who was counting, I'd like to know.)

When I'm anxious (before a major talk or sermon, for instance), frightened, uptight, spiritually dry, or being tempted, I've found the Jesus prayer calls me to a humble reliance on God. I have found it does, indeed, help me to "practice God's presence." It has all the elements of a proper prayer, recognizing Jesus as Lord, asking humbly for his assistance and mercy, and admitting sin. The purest form of prayer addresses the Father in Jesus' name. But the Jesus prayer is a reminder that Jesus is Lord, that I'm a sinner, and that I need his mercy.

Secret Acts of Devotion

It was a cold December night. The next day would bring Christmas Eve. I snuck out of my house, put on a coat, grabbed my bag, and headed outside. A youth outside in the dead of night usually means trouble, or at least toilet paper on the trees. I had done my share of that, but this time my intention was different. I wanted to give a present to Jesus.

Earlier that day, I had picked out a ham from a local grocery store. I wrote "Merry Christmas" on the bag and now left it on the front porch of a financially strapped family who had lost their father to an affair just a few months earlier. Until now, many years after the fact, I've never told anybody about this act. I was practicing my first secret act of devotion. (Now I guess I've lost one!)

I like to encourage all Christians, but especially those who are predominantly contemplatives, to engage in "secret acts of devotion." A secret act of devotion is something you do—giving an anonymous gift, helping out someone "behind the scenes," sending a card— without letting anyone, even the person who benefits, know you had anything to do with it.

The importance of secrecy is that it ensures that you are doing it for the love of God, and the love of God only. Any intimate relationship has its secrets; a husband and wife share things with each other that they will never share with anyone else. In our relationship—and romance—with God, part of the intimacy is to share secrets with him. On God's end, these secrets may be something he has shared with us or done for us that we are not to share with anyone else. (Jesus once healed a man and told him not to tell anyone about it—Mark 8:26; see also 8:30.) On our end, it could be a service we perform that no one will ever know about. Some secret acts of devotion might include:

> An anonymous gift of cash to someone in need
> A poem or letter written to God, then burned
> A song sung only in the presence of God
> A "secret" walk or night vigil taken in the presence of God
> A secret devotional place where you frequently go
>   to meet God
> Intensive, intercessory prayer and fasting
> A vow to give up something permanently or for a period
>   of time to signify how your most important needs are
>   met in God
> A symbol of your love for God, which you carry in your
>   pocket or wear as a necklace or ring
> Working "behind the scenes" to help an unemployed person
>   get a job
> Sending an anonymous note of encouragement to a pastor
>   or friend
> Planting a tree or sowing wildflower seeds in a field to
>   celebrate God the Creator

With practice, you'll think of many other secret acts of devotion on your own.

Dancing Prayer

By "dancing" I don't mean bodily movements, although some contemplatives may find such activity meaningful; rather, I mean that, just as the woman traditionally allows the man to lead in ballroom dancing, so we allow God to lead in our prayers.

Vigorous intercession, wrestling in prayer, and laying our requests before God all have a place. But allowing God to speak and place requests before us also has a place. Dancing prayer is prayer in which we allow God to lead; it is presumptuous to assume that we even know what most needs to be prayed about; how necessary it is, then, to let God take the lead.

> *Vigorous intercession, wrestling in prayer, and laying our requests before God all have a place. But allowing God to speak and place requests before us also has a place.*

This may mean our prayer time leads us to repentance, celebration, intercession, introspection, or any number of things. The important element in dancing prayer is to be still enough so that God can lead, like a good dancer, as we pray.

To nurture my relationship with God, I must learn to hear his voice, learn to adopt his concerns, and seek to know his perspective. There are times when I absolutely must pour out my heart to him, but I never want my prayer life to lapse into a monologue.

Sit with this image: dancing with God—and let the Holy Spirit lead you as you pray.

Centering Prayer

It is particularly difficult to describe this type of prayer in writing, as it is best taught in person. In general, however, centering prayer works like this: Choose a word (*Jesus* or *Father,* for example) as a focus for contemplative prayer. Repeat the word silently in your mind for a set amount of time (say, twenty minutes) until your heart seems to be repeating the word by itself, just as naturally and involuntarily as breathing. As your mind is filled with thoughts of Jesus or the Father or another appropriate subject (love, joy, or peace) you are protected from outside distractions.

It is hard to describe this to the western mind. We think, "Well, what do I do next?" But centering prayer is a contemplative act in which you don't do anything; you're simply resting in the presence of God. Focusing on God the Father, Son, or Holy Spirit, or the beauty of the Trinity, helps you to have a centering anchor for your contemplation, so your thoughts don't race around looking for more stimulation. As thoughts drift, you simply repeat the word in your heart, centering once again, to bring you back to focus.

Some Christian traditions might view our anxious and wordy prayers as distracting rather than effective. John Climacus (late sixth to early seventh century), who wrote an early classic on the Christian life, put it this way: "Let there be no studied elegance in the words of your prayer . . . do not launch out into long discourses that fritter away your mind in efforts for eloquence. One word alone spoken by the Publican touched God's mercy; a single word full of faith saved the Good Thief. Many words in prayer often fill the mind with images and distract it, while often one single word draws it into recollection."[17]

The purpose of centering prayer is not to cultivate feelings or create a "spiritual experience"; it is simply to rest in and enjoy the blessed presence of God. For those who question this, we need merely look to the human example—the deepest kind of love is often that which allows you to rest in another's presence without saying or doing anything, just enjoying being together. If a husband can feel this way with his wife, or a sister with her sibling, or a mother with her infant, why can't Christians enjoy this with their God?

> *The deepest kind of love is often that which allows you to rest in another's presence without saying or doing anything, just enjoying being together.*

Prayer of the Heart

The challenge of contemplatives is to move beyond the purely intellectual exercise that makes up ninety to one hundred percent of our prayers. When we westerners think of "prayer," most of us think of us talking to God. Other Christians have found, however, that there is a prayer of the heart that, while not replacing prayer of the mind, is an essential ingredient of a full life of prayer.

God created us with more than intellectual or cerebral faculties, yet we do little to develop the emotional element of our being. One writer describes it this way: "Never would we come to true peace and fulfillment if only our cerebral faculties were involved in conversing with God. And yet it is a fact that, in comparison with the overwhelming rational and cognitive training, we receive very little education in our emotional growth. Often the affective dimension of adults is either infantile or of a crudity which is neighbor to a barbarian attitude."[18]

Prayer of the heart does not call us to abandon our mind; that would be as silly as much of our praying that abandons the heart. But it does call us to use the mind to focus on our heart. What are we feeling as we enter God's presence? Is our adoration centered on God, or something else? Are we content to enjoy the presence of God, or are we too restless to quiet the mind for just a few minutes?

That our faith must not be ruled by our feelings does not mean that feelings are irrelevant or even unimportant. God created our emotions for a purpose. It is true that we cannot entirely trust them, but it is also true that we shut off part of our true selves if we entirely ignore them.

Prayer of the heart then, like centering prayer, is more "being" prayer than "doing" prayer. Its aim is not to get an answer from God, make a request known to God, receive an insight from God, or even express our commitment to God. Rather, the prayer of the heart focuses on emotional attachment to, or adoration of, God. It develops and matures the affective faculty of our souls that is so frequently crippled in our society. Its aim is to love God, to have our hearts enlarged so that God owns more and more of us. Centering prayer focuses on being with, and aware of, God.

Stations of the Cross

Remembering the stations of the cross has historically been a popular method of contemplation. Christians simply pray through the various events surrounding Christ's crucifixion, perhaps beginning with Gethsemane and moving on from there: the sentence of death given to Jesus, Jesus receiving his cross, Jesus falling, Simon helping Jesus carry the cross, Jesus falling a second time, women mourning for Jesus, Jesus falling again, Jesus being stripped of his clothing, Jesus being nailed to the cross, Jesus calling out to John and Mary, Jesus dying on the cross, Jesus being taken down from the cross, Jesus being laid in the tomb.

At each point pause and picture the truth of the Scripture in your mind. What was going on? What can you learn from Christ's sacrifice and obedience? There are no set prayers for each station, so let the Holy Spirit lead you in your prayers (and don't forget to enjoy the glory of the resurrection!).

Praying through the stations will give your contemplative prayers concrete structure while also allowing spontaneous insight and petitions.

Meditative Prayer

Ignatius of Loyola, in *The Spiritual Exercises,* helped to make mental prayer more popular. His book provides several different examples of mental or contemplative prayer, and those who are particularly interested in this type of prayer would do well to buy a copy of this classic.

Ignatius talks about prayerful reflection of a biblical text, prayerful reflection of a particular theme, or prayerful use of an object (something you can see, taste, touch, hear, or smell), reflecting on its practical lessons. Each time of prayer should begin with humble submission of the will to God and be concluded by returning to God in a genuine personal encounter.

> *Relationships, including our relationship with God, are dynamic. The exercises I have mentioned have proven helpful in the lives of other Christians, but the exciting truth is that all Christians can build their own stories in the journey of loving God.*

These types of prayers may seem new—and somewhat uncom- fortable—to some. The difficulty of writing about them could be imagined if someone assigned you the topic, "How to fall in love." Relationships, including our relationship with God, are dynamic. The exercises I have mentioned have proven helpful in the lives of other Christians, but the exciting truth is that all Christians can build their own stories in the journey of loving God.

The Temptations of Contemplatives

Losing Balance

In our healthy desire to find our joy and love in God, we can sometimes limit how God can reveal his love. God wants us to delight in him, yes; but he also wants us to delight in the people and the world he has made. Contemplatives sometimes make the mistake of creating a secular/sacred dichotomy in which their love for God precludes enjoying the company of others or something God has made.

Healthy contemplatives will understand that rich human relationships are a way to enjoy God's love, just as is solitary and intimate prayer. Good music, the beauty of the outdoors, art, and recreation all contain mini-celebrations of God as Creator so we can love God while appreciating the wonder of his creation.

> *God is always God, and we are always human and "never the 'twain shall meet." We can relate to God, but we cannot be absorbed into God.*

Don't exclude the enjoyment of things other than God in your zeal to love God more passionately. God can reveal himself to us just as much in a conversation with a fellow believer as he can when we are on our knees in prayer.

Absorbing the Ego

Some forms of contemplation wander from the folds of orthodox Christianity, and contemplatives must watch out for these. In particular we should beware of any meditation that calls our ego to somehow be absorbed into God rather than talking about relating to God. God is always God, and we are always human and "never the 'twain shall meet." We can relate to God, but we cannot be absorbed into God. Such foolishness is not Christian thinking.

Be wary of practices that speak of simply "emptying" yourself and creating a vacuum. A Christian wants to be filled with the Holy Spirit, not emptied out. Jesus spoke of a man being delivered of a demon, yet being worse off because, remaining empty, he was soon inhabited by a legion of demons.[19]

Forgetting Virtue

Historically the contemplative role has grown out of asceticism for this reason: Great mystics have held that there is no progress in faith without a lessening of vice. We cannot gaze on the glorious face of God while lusting in our heart after the world's sinful pleasures. Contemplatives must grow beyond an adolescent infatuation to incorporate self-discipline and self-control. Just as marriage must pull two people beyond a crush to engage in a commitment built on self-sacrifice, so contemplatives must move beyond mere meditation (the failure of some Eastern and faddish religions) to an alignment of our will and obedience into conformity with Christ.

Getting Addicted to Spiritual Experience

The ancients viewed contemplation as a foretaste of heavenly joys; it was rarely described as something that can be expected to continue indefinitely on earth. Spiritual feelings can be so intense—Augustine once described them as a "holy inebriation"—that we don't want to let them go. Contemplatives will have to accept that just as earthly bodies have their limits, so earthly souls and emotions have their limits, too. We should be thankful for the spiritual joys we receive but also tolerant of their transient nature. We must also beware of "spiritual gluttony" in which we begin seeking the feelings instead of God.[20]

Are You a Contemplative?

Are you a contemplative? Score the following statements on a scale of five to one, with five being very true and one being not true at all. Record your answer in the space provided.

_____ 1. I feel closest to God when my emotions are awakened, when God quietly touches my heart, tells me that he loves me, and makes me feel like I'm his closest friend. I would rather be alone with God, contemplating his love, than participating in a formal liturgy or being distracted by a walk outside.

_____ 2. The most difficult times in my faith are when I can't feel God's presence within me.

_____ 3. The words *lover, intimacy,* and *heart* are very appealing to me.

_____ 4. I really enjoy having thirty minutes of uninterrupted time a day to sit in quiet prayer and "hold hands" with God, writing love letters to him and enjoying his presence.

_____ 5. I would enjoy reading *The Transforming Friendship.*

_____ 6. When I think of God, I think of love, friendship, and adoration more than anything else.

The total of all your answers. _____

Any score of fifteen or higher indicates a preference for this spiritual temperament. Please take a moment now to register this score in chapter eleven on page 217 so you will have a composite picture of your soul's path to God.

The Message of Contemplatives

As I grew up, it seemed to me that the "giants" of the Christian faith were the men and women who had accomplished great things for God: the great leaders, authors, preachers, and servants. Their degrees, accomplishments, and résumés were long and elaborate affairs. Perhaps they had started entire movements or led people by the tens of thousands to experience salvation. You could "judge" a person's sanctity by how long it took to introduce them before they spoke.

Contemplatives point us in an entirely new direction. All our work may seem absolutely essential to us, but I wonder if that isn't just because we have an inflated view of our own importance. Or perhaps our work is more of an attempt to validate our own existence than to truly love God.

Contemplatives remind us of a startling fact: There is one thing that each individual Christian can do that nobody else can: give our personal love and affection to God. God can raise up plenty of evangelists, teachers, writers, and witnesses, but only I can give my personal love and affection to God. My spouse, pastor, or coworker can't do this for me—only I can give God this love, a love that he wants very much.

Imagine that you had six children. Five of them loved you dearly, sent you cards and letters on a regular basis, and made sure you were frequently reminded of their devotion. The other child left several years ago, telling you, "I hate you and never want to see you again. As far as I'm concerned, I don't have any parents." Would the love of the five ever completely erase the pain you'd feel over the alienation of that one rebellious child? Certainly not. Amazingly, it's the same with God. Just because he has my wife's devotion and Billy Graham's devotion doesn't mean he doesn't desire mine. And I'm the only person who can give him *my* love and adoration.

> *There is one thing that each individual Christian can do that nobody else can: give our personal love and affection to God.*

Contemplatives and mystics will perhaps always be looked at askance because their service to God is so very private, but this private love is so cherished by God. M. Basil Pennington described it this way:

> I have run into a situation in marriage counseling a number of times. The couple is unhappy. The wife is dissatisfied and the husband cannot see why. He goes into a long recital of all he is doing for her. He is holding down two or three jobs, building a new house, buying her everything. But to all this the wife quietly replies: If only he would stop for a few minutes and give me himself! I sometimes think that God, as He sees us rushing about in all our doing of good, says to Himself: If only they would stop for a few minutes and give me themselves![21]

It's up to each of us to love God with this fervor.

TEN

INTELLECTUALS: LOVING GOD WITH THE MIND

No, no, no," the pastor said, shaking his head. "I'm sure it was located in the northwest corner."

"I'm sorry," the other pastor said, the one who was driving the car, "but I've always held to the southeastern view."

The first pastor looked at his atlas one more time. "No, couldn't be," he said, pointing to a location near the southeast corner. "It has to be here," and his finger moved up the map.

It was hard not to smile as our car pointed north. It was a hot, summer day and we were headed to a denominational convention where we would make a joint presentation. As other cars passed, I could imagine the discussions—the latest baseball scores, perhaps, or the most recent business mergers, or maybe some Hollywood gossip. I felt reasonably certain, however, that not one carload in a million could possibly guess what was being discussed by the men in our car: a heart-stopping debate on the location of the sheepgate in ancient Jerusalem!

These somewhat silly discussions partly explain why so much disdain is often cast on intellectual pursuit in some sectors of the church. We've probably all heard someone say, with great condescension in their voice, "So and so's faith is all in their head." But the truth is, Christ himself exalted the role of the intellect when he urged us to love the Lord our God with all our heart, soul, *mind,* and strength.

It is difficult for some enthusiasts and contemplatives to understand how powerfully some of us can be drawn to the Lord through a stimulated mind. When intellectuals' minds are awakened, when they understand something new about God or his ways with his children, then their adoration is unleashed.

Just as the contemplative can spend hours basking in the presence of God, so an intellectual can spend long seasons contemplating a challenging verse or concept. One time, I was deep in the book of Job and was suddenly caught short when I read verses 6–8 in chapter 35: "If you sin, how does that affect him? If your sins are many, what does that do to him? If you are righteous, what do you give to him, or what does he receive from your hand? Your wickedness affects only a man like yourself, and your righteousness only the sons of men."

Our culture doesn't always think of the mind when it thinks of love and devotion. Drugstores don't sell chocolate brains on Valentine's Day—it's always the heart that is exalted when love is talked about—but biblically speaking, chocolate brains would be perfectly acceptable.

I knew that something precious was behind those words; at first, I wasn't sure what the passage was getting at, but I knew something was there, and the verses provided many pleasant reflections and meditations in the days ahead.

I've found that for me to be growing in Christ, I need to have my mind stimulated with Scriptures such as the above. I need to be challenged and face "the love of hard questions," as my friend John Rankin likes to say. If I'm not learning new things about God, my relationship with him feels stagnant.

Many of the books in the New Testament (the epistles of John, Galatians, and Jude, for example) make especially strong contentions for right thinking as well as right living. Intellectuals remind us of the high calling of loving God with our mind. Our culture doesn't always think of the mind when it thinks of love and devotion. Drugstores don't sell chocolate brains on Valentine's Day—it's always the heart that is exalted when love is talked about—but biblically speaking, chocolate brains would be perfectly acceptable. The Bible is emphatic that our mind is one of the key elements that we can use to love God.

Intellectual pursuit and service have played a key role in the advancement of God's work. One writer has pointed out that the main reason the early church was so successful in its witness to the pagan world was that it not only outlived and out-died the world, it also out-thought it.[1] Though the great Christian thinkers shared fundamental disagreements with each other, luminaries such as Augustine, Calvin, Erasmus, Aquinas, Pascal, and others have helped Christianity not only keep up with scholarship but advance it. It would be difficult to overestimate the influence of scholasticism on the history of Christianity. Building on Augustine's foundational work from the fourth century, it was largely the Theology of Scholasticism that crowned the High Middle Ages and led the church out of the Dark Ages. The powerful thought that fueled the Reformation would soon follow.

> *Any form of Christianity ... that rejects or even denigrates the importance of the mind is not a biblical Christianity.*

Thomas Aquinas, the great theologian of the High Middle Ages (many Reformed theologians like to believe that Aquinas' thought was in line with the reformational thinking that would follow), put this aspect of history in perspective when he argued that, according to 1 Timothy 2:1, prayer in every case must include, among other things, *an ascent of the mind to God.*[2]

Any form of Christianity, then, that rejects or even denigrates the importance of the mind is not a biblical Christianity.

The Biblical View of Intellectuals

Have you ever seen a pulpit with the carved-wood image of an eagle on it? The ornate pulpit is symbolically proclaiming the truth that the Word of God destroys the work of Satan. Eagles are the natural predators of the serpent. Throughout the ages, and indeed throughout Scripture itself, the proclamation of God's Word is given high priority as an essential component in waging war against the powers of darkness.

When Moses blessed the tribe of Levi, he blessed a tribe that "teaches your precepts to Jacob and your law to Israel."[3] The Levites were released from other duties so they could function in the one duty of studying and teaching—loving God with the mind.

Biblical individuals also fulfilled this role. The Bible is clear that "Solomon showed his love for the LORD."[4] One of the ways he loved God was by using his intellect to the glory of God. It's particularly interesting to note that Solomon didn't limit his mind to religious words of wisdom; he also explored the natural world, for God is the natural Creator of all. "[Solomon] described plant life, from the cedar of Lebanon to the hyssop that grows out of walls. He also taught about animals and birds, reptiles and fish. Men of all nations came to listen to Solomon's wisdom, sent by all the kings of the world, who had heard of his wisdom."[5]

A professor of biology can love God with his mind every bit as much as a professor of systematic theology. Since God created all, any study that explores, examines, and explains the natural world can shed some light on the nature of our God and help us to know him better.

Words of wisdom can be an active part of worship, or, as in the case of Psalm 49, a call to worship:

> Hear this, all you peoples;
> listen, all who live in this world,
> both low and high,
> rich and poor alike:
> My mouth will speak words of wisdom;
> the utterance from my heart will give understanding.
> I will turn my ear to a proverb;
> with the harp I will expound my riddle.[6]

The sermon is a crucial part of the general church service. It does not follow or precede worship—it *is* worship.

A good part of the book of Proverbs also stresses how important a trained mind is for us to love God:

> Let the wise listen and add to their learning,
>   and let the discerning get guidance—
> for understanding proverbs and parables,
>   the sayings and riddles of the wise.
> The fear of the LORD is the beginning of knowledge,
>   but fools despise wisdom and discipline.[7]

Proverbs tells us to "cry aloud for understanding" and to "search for it as for hidden treasure."[8] We are told that "wisdom is supreme; therefore get wisdom. Though it cost all you have, get understanding."[9] Right thinking—conforming our thoughts to the thoughts of God—enables right living.

We need to pause and remember how radical this is. Our culture tells us to seek fame and fortune, affluence and power. Scripture tells us our first search, our primary calling, is to get wisdom and understanding.

Jesus himself revealed intellectual tendencies. At twelve years old, he was found discussing the law in the temple.[10] Teaching was a large part of his ministry. Though he was forceful in his denunciation of intellectual contrivances that kept people from God, Jesus understood that the mind, as well as the heart, had to be transformed. He urged his followers to love God with all their mind.[11]

> *Though he was forceful in his denunciation of intellectual contrivances that kept people from God, Jesus understood that the mind, as well as the heart, had to be transformed.*

Are we doing that? Are we earnestly seeking to chase out all our wrong notions of God, and offer up to him a mind that has been fully redeemed?

Intellectual Training

The first time I drove by Regent College, I went right past it without realizing it. At the time, Regent was housed in a couple of converted fraternity houses, just off the University of British Columbia campus. The bookstore was stationed in a portable trailer. What I knew of Regent, I knew from the professors who taught there—professors like Dr. Bruce Waltke and Dr. J. I. Packer. I had no idea they could teach in a place like this. Regent has undergone massive physical transformation, but the lack of physical facilities in the early days didn't really bother us in the mid-eighties. It was the teaching and relationships that kept us coming back. I remember when my classmates and I began graduating and breaking up to go our separate ways. One friend who I often ate and studied with left a note for me on my books as he departed from "campus" for the last time. We both knew the likelihood of our meeting again was very small. He was heading off to teach at a United Methodist school in Canada; I was returning to life in the States. Another friend was going back to Hong Kong, hoping to prepare Christians there for the return of the country to Chinese control. Another friend—who had been sobered but strengthened by having his paper virtually torn to shreds during a seminar—was preparing to become a pastor in the Vancouver area.

As I walked around the school for the last time, I was in awe of what had been accomplished over the past two or three years in so many lives. Men and women were leaving as very different people. Our minds had been provoked, our hearts had been challenged, and now we were ready to begin our own feeble efforts aimed at accomplishing the same thing with others. This same process continues unabated today. In countries around the world, the Christian church is advancing itself with education aimed at training the Christian mind. It's a thrilling reality and a deep source of strength for the professing church.

While I believe everybody can gain from such an experience, intellectuals will especially derive great benefit from getting formal theological training. A good school will equip you to further educate yourself once you've graduated, but there is no substitute for first establishing a solid foundation.

This is getting easier and easier to do. If the two or three years required for a master's degree just aren't feasible, consider taking just one year off from work and getting a one-year degree. Regent

College in Vancouver, B.C., has an excellent one-year program of study. You might also consider taking summer classes—many seminaries and Bible colleges offer one-week courses that accumulate credit toward a one-year degree. These one-week courses can give you enough to study for an entire year if you take the time to draw up a list of related books that you'd like to read in the months following the course.

Think how much stronger you'd be as a Christian if you picked one topic a year for in-depth study. In just a few years, you could be quite conversant on a number of important truths. It's clear that the church would be a vastly stronger institution if we applied ourselves with a little more fervor to developing the mind that God has given us.

> I don't remember a single traffic or weather report that has changed the course of my life or redirected me into God's purpose. However, by spending a year listening to the men and women to whom God has given great insight, I can become a better person.

If time and expense forbid you from actually attending a school, you can always consider extension classes through audio or video. You can start small study classes at your church using the videotaped lectures of prominent professors. It's always helpful to study in a group dynamic; I've found discussion to be an invaluable method of honing my own thoughts and beliefs.

If others around you lack interest, however, you can turn your work commute into a rich time of study using audiotapes in your car. Two of the best sources for these video classes and audiocassette tapes are Regent College, 5800 University Blvd., Vancouver, B.C. V6T 2E4; and Ligonier Ministries, P.O. Box 547500, Orlando, FL 32854. Regent has a more diversified faculty than Ligonier, which is strongly reformed in its theology, but both have excellent courses at surprisingly affordable prices.

You can spend a year's worth of commutes listening to talk-show hosts spout off on the latest issues, but if you do that, you'll be unchanged at the end of the year. In all the years I've commuted to work, I don't remember a single traffic or weather report that has changed the course of my life or redirected me into God's purpose. However, by spending a year listening to the men and women to whom God has given great insight, I can become a better person.

The Disciplines

Intellectuals should aim to broaden their faith by gaining an understanding of the basic disciplines of theological training. These disciplines include church history, biblical studies, systematic theology, ethics, and apologetics. A full seminary education would also include a few other disciplines, but these five comprise a good start toward building an informed Christian mind.

Numerous books discuss each of these disciplines, though you may not find many in a local Christian bookstore. A pastor who has been to seminary should be able to meet with you and within a few minutes make several suggestions. As you begin reading, you'll come across footnotes and endnotes that will direct you to similar volumes. To get started, you might consider the following.

Church History

Church history contains numerous compelling and true stories of great faith, commitment, and devotion. Even more, it connects the head to the heart. It's one thing to read the passionate words of men or women dedicated to evangelism; it's another to read that they went to a foreign country as missionaries with their belongings in a casket because they didn't expect to live more than eighteen months in the new climate.

When the writer of Proverbs wrote that there is nothing new under the sun, he was foreseeing the growth and development of the church. Over its two-thousand-year history, the church has faced the same heresies under many different names. The church has also overcome many of the same struggles and dealt with the same issues of reaction and then balance. A man or woman who has a broad understanding of church history would be a valuable addition to any church's leadership.[12]

Latourette's two volumes entitled *History of Christianity*[13] have been standard fare in seminaries and Bible colleges for a number of years, though they may be a bit lengthy for many with a passing interest. Another work, *Two Kingdoms: The Church and Culture Through the Ages*,[14] is gaining some well-deserved notice.

Eerdmans' Handbook to the History of Christianity is a reader-friendly volume. Clyde Manschreck has compiled original documents in his two-volume series entitled *A History of Christianity: Readings in the History of the Church*. *The Pelican History of the Church*, a series, also has some very helpful works, and these are small paperbacks, which can easily be carried wherever you're headed.

Apart from these introductions, you can find many books dealing with a particular segment of church history. North American readers might be interested in Daniel Reid's *Dictionary of Christianity in America*,[15] Mark Noll's *A History of Christianity in the United States and Canada*,[16] or David Wells' *Eerdmans' Handbook to Christianity in America*.[17]

Church history is an essential foundation upon which to build the theological mind. Trying to understand theology without church history is like trying to understand world events by reading headlines and ignoring the articles. You'll have an idea of what everything is all about, but little idea of what it all means.

Biblical Studies

I wish there were some way I could make the page begin dancing for you right now to signal the importance of this particular section. In the absence of a CD-ROM, however, let me state that I believe ninety percent of the

> *Ninety percent of the difficulty in the Christian life is caused because we don't understand the Scriptures well enough.*

difficulty in the Christian life is caused because we don't understand the Scriptures well enough. Ninety percent. Biblical studies, I believe, are that crucial.

Broadly speaking, we can divide biblical studies into three components: reading through Scripture, meticulous study of portions of Scripture (often referred to as "exegesis"), and reading books that help us understand what Scripture says. It's a good practice for every Christian to have some type of program to regularly read through the Bible, whether it's once a year or once every three years. This doesn't mean we have to start at Genesis and conclude with Revelation. I've tried a number of different approaches. You can read one Old Testament book—Genesis, for example—and then one New Testament book—Matthew. Then go back and read Exodus, and follow that up with Mark, and so on. Since there are approximately twice as many Old Testament books as New Testament books, I've found a helpful schedule that begins with Genesis, Psalms, and Matthew, and then follows each book in its order—Exodus, Proverbs, Mark, and so on. This splits up the Gospels and some of the more difficult Old Testament accounts.

I can't tell you how many times God has providentially placed something before me that I really needed to hear at just the time I read it. A regular reading program gives God a great tool to speak truth into our hearts. I haven't met a single Christian who reads Scripture daily who isn't enthusiastic about its effects.

If you think you might be an intellectual in your spiritual temperament, *this* is the place to start. Begin reading Scripture *daily*. Even if you're not an intellectual, daily Scripture reading should be a part of every Christian's life.

We'll also benefit from moving beyond straight reading to giving careful study to particular passages. An excellent book to prepare us for this work is *How to Read the Bible for All It's Worth* by Gordon Fee and Douglas Stuart. Another helpful book in this regard is *Knowing Scripture* by R. C. Sproul.

As you begin studying individual books, you might want to consult a few good commentaries and then add some other books on the cultural history of the time period about which you're studying, including Bible dictionaries and atlases. Your aim is to better your understanding of what individual passages actually mean and teach.

There are sixty-six books in the Bible. If we start devoting six months a year or so to turning a book of the Bible inside out, meticulously studying every passage, reading the commentaries that relate to it, and doing our best to really understand it, most of us can thoroughly study the entire Bible in our lifetime.

Systematic Theology

Systematic theology is the study of Christian doctrines—salvation, baptism, church order, and the like. There are two excellent books to begin with—J. I. Packer's *Concise Theology* and R. C. Sproul's *Essential Truths of the Christian Faith*. Both of these volumes provide introductory or refresher samplers of Christian doctrine.

As you move out from these two volumes, you're going to find particular theological bents within each systematic theology. There are the classics—Aquinas' *Summa Theologica* and Calvin's *Institutes of Christian Religion*, among many others—and your pastor can also help you find a good one- or multi-volume work that will explain the beliefs of your own tradition.

There are seven basic topics in systematic theology: God, humankind, Jesus, the Holy Spirit, the Church, eschatology (last things), and revelation. In addition to general collections of systematic theologies, you can read volumes that focus on just one of these topics—the church (Chuck Colson's *The Body*, for instance), or the nature of God (J. I. Packer's *Knowing God* or R. C. Sproul's *The Holiness of God*).

Ethics

Christianity is about what we believe, but it is also about how we behave; and the study of Christian ethics seeks to provide a framework from which Christians can make prayerful decisions. Ethics seeks to answer the question from the Old Testament, which Francis Schaeffer made famous: "How shall we then live?"

A man who has a significant prison ministry told me he has yet to meet a rapist or murderer who isn't convinced he is on his way to heaven. "I believe Jesus is God, of course I'm going to heaven," they'll tell him, and yet show little remorse for their previous actions. The study of ethics reminds us of the need and reality of Christian transformation. Salvation is about more than missing hell; it's about being transformed—*changed*—here on earth.

To develop this aspect of your intellect, you might consider John Jefferson Davies' relatively recent introduction entitled *Evangelical Ethics*. You might also consider John Murray's *Principles of Conduct,* or the classic *The Abolition of Man* by C. S. Lewis.

> *A man who has a significant prison ministry told me he has yet to meet a rapist or murderer who isn't convinced he is on his way to heaven.*

Besides the general introductory volumes just mentioned, you might also want to consider some volumes that focus on one issue, such as poverty, sexual ethics, and the like.

As time moves on, Christians need to be actively and increasingly engaged in social issues, not only for our own benefit, but the benefit of society as a whole. Technology is opening up entirely new avenues of ethical discussion: When does life begin? How do we know when natural life ends? Can a nuclear war ever be considered a "just war"? How do we live responsibly in a world where so many are in need?

These are questions many Christians face on a daily basis. We need those with a particular intellectual bent to present the issues, suggest some guidelines, and help us understand Scripture and God's will on the matter.

Apologetics

When I used to commute to work, I liked to pass my commuting time by listening to tapes. I figured it extended my day by about two hours. Rather than passing time, I was able to use it. One tape in particular got me excited like few others have. It was the tape of a "Mars Hill Forum" featuring a Christian pastor, John Rankin, debating Patricia Ireland, head of the National Organization for Women.

Reverend Rankin did a superlative job, winning over a hostile crowd at Smith College. His ability to explain the truth and excellence of Christian beliefs in a very secular arena left me in stunned awe. I have a great deal of respect for those who can present the Christian faith in an effective manner.

Sometimes God can call us out of our comfort zones, and we need to be ready. Not long after I listened to Reverend Rankin's tape, a group of students at Swarthmore College asked me to come and do an evangelistic talk on Jesus' view of women. I've never seen myself as a particularly effective apologist, and I tried to talk the leaders into inviting John Rankin; but one of the students had heard me speak somewhere else and was adamant on having me come. I prayed about it further, and finally accepted.

When you're used to speaking to Christians, it's a challenge to face a crowd that is looking for every weak point it can find. These are the types of discussions usually known as "apologetics." Apologetics concerns how we explain and defend the faith today in the midst of unbelief. It also involves defending true Christian doctrine in the face of heresy, especially as it comes from Christian or non-Christian cults. I call these two branches of apologetics "external" and "internal" apologetics. The former defends the faith against those who believe Christianity is untrue; the latter defends it from those who claim to be Christian but who hold to teachings that are contrary to true Christian doctrine.

Two contemporary (though getting dated) classics in apologetics are Paul Little's *Know Why You Believe* and Josh McDowell's *Evidence That Demands a Verdict*. Evangelist and apologist Ravi Zacharias is rapidly becoming the leading apologist among evangelicals. His book *Can Man Live Without God?* challenges Christians to answer tough questions with relevance and intellectual excellence.

Peter Kreeft's and Ronald Tacelli's *Handbook of Christian Apologetics* has been described as a "virtual one-volume, self-study course on essential apologetics," and James Sire uses college-tested material to help university students address the nature of belief and other questions in *Why Should Anyone Believe Anything at All?*

For a history of apologetics, you might check out *Classical Reading in Christian Apologetics, A.D. 100–1800*, edited by Russ Bush. Introductory works to consider include William Lane Craig's *Apologetics: An Introduction* and Norman Geisler's *Christian Apologetics*.

For a positive example of a contemporary apologist, I'd encourage you to listen to some of the Mars Hills Forums featuring John Rankin. His tapes are available through the Theological Education Institute, www.therankinfile.com. John was trained at Gordon-Conwell Theological Seminary and the Harvard Divinity School, so his presentations are not only spiritually sensitive, but also well-researched and reasoned.

Creeds

Before he died, Dr. Klaus Bockmuehl, a professor at Regent College, often remarked that we need to be reminded of some doctrines every twenty minutes. Creeds help us do that and thus can be powerful tools for spiritual growth. Creeds also reveal the lie in the popular but misguided phrase, "So long as we do the right thing, it doesn't matter what we believe." How do we know what the right thing is if we don't know what we believe? Once we dispense with creeds, dogmas, or certain beliefs, we lose our ability to determine if what we are doing is right; then we can be pulled into the diabolical practice of serving Satan while we think we're serving God.[18]

> *We need to be reminded of some doctrines every twenty minutes.*

As much as we may wince when we talk about the importance of creeds—"that heady stuff," as some might say—intellectuals remind us that they play a crucial role in the advancement of the church. Dorothy Sayers, a popular British writer during the second world war, penned some words that remain as relevant today as when they were first written:

> It is worse than useless for Christians to talk about the importance of Christian morality, unless they are prepared to take their stand upon the fundamentals of Christian theology. It is a lie to say that dogma does not matter; it matters enormously. It is fatal to let people suppose that Christianity is only a mode of feeling; it is vitally necessary

to insist that it is first and foremost a rational explanation of the universe. It is hopeless to offer Christianity as a vaguely idealistic aspiration of a simple and consoling kind; it is, on the contrary, a hard, tough, exacting, and complex doctrine, steeped in a drastic and uncompromising realism. And it is fatal to imagine that everybody knows quite well what Christianity is and needs only a little encouragement to practice it. The brutal fact is that . . . not one person in a hundred has the faintest notion what the Church teaches about God or man or society or the person of Jesus Christ.[19]

What we believe about God will affect how we serve him, in the same way that what we believe about a person will affect how we treat that person. I remember sitting next to a rather humble-looking man during a lunch break at a conference. We were having a pleasant chat, but in the back of my mind something was bothering me. He looked familiar, but I couldn't place him. His name tag had just his first name on it. All of a sud-

Doctrine affects our actions as surely as eyeglasses affect our sight.

den it hit me, and I realized I was talking to a former United States senator. "Would you happen to be . . . ," I asked, and mentioned his full name.

"As a matter of fact, yes," the senator said, "but don't tell anybody."

Immediately, those close enough to hear what was going on changed their demeanor. This man in casual clothes suddenly received a new measure of respect. People were more careful with their words. It was interesting to watch the way people started acting differently during that lunch and then later as the conference progressed and others also discovered who he was. Ideally, we may not always act this way, but even the apostle Paul had respect for certain positions. In one instance, he responds rather glibly to a fellow, only to apologize when he is told that the man he has been glib with happens to be the high priest.[20]

In a similar way, what we know about God will affect how we treat him. If we view our Creator as just a "good buddy" or as a harsh taskmaster and vindictive judge, our lives will be shaped accordingly. Doctrine affects our actions as surely as eyeglasses affect our sight. Thus creeds are essential to help us love God as God deserves to be loved.

Today's intellectuals serve God by explaining what the Christian faith is and what the Christian faith means. Both parts are essential. Jesus is God (this is a crucial statement of faith), but what does this mean for my life?

Creeds are collections of these statements of belief. They may or may not be exhaustive. The Nicene Creed is a foundational creed of Christianity, but this creed doesn't, for instance, cover every point of belief that Christians need to understand.

There are "ecumenical" creeds which were designed for and are accepted by the entire visible church, and "domestic" creeds written for particular segments of the church—Presbyterianism or Roman Catholicism, for instance. Intellectuals may want to become familiar with the major creeds, even if they are not a part of his or her tradition. The Apostles' Creed, the Nicene Creed, the Athanasian Creed, the Augsburg Confession, and the Westminster Confession together comprise a good start. For further study, consult P. Schaff's three-volume work, *Creeds of Christendom,* or J. N. D. Kelly's *Early Christian Creeds*.

Developing as an Intellectual

If you score high as an intellectual on the spiritual temperament test, or even if you just want to begin building your mind as a way to love God, choose a discipline that carries the most interest for you. Are you drawn to the challenges of apologetics, or are you the type of person who will be most inspired by the stories of Christian history? Do you need to brush up on your general knowledge of the Bible, or do you need to begin applying your faith in the area of ethics?

This is a lifetime calling. We have as long as God gives us on this earth to begin handing our minds over, bit by bit, to the truth of God. By the time I die, I want my actions, my thoughts, and my beliefs to all conform to the image of Christ. This won't happen by accident.

Fortunately, we have a great Teacher, the Holy Spirit, and a reliable and authoritative group of teachings, the Bible, to help us accomplish that aim.

The Temptations of Intellectuals
Loving Controversy

Timothy may have been an intellectual who loved controversy. Paul's two letters to Timothy contain several strong exhortations to avoid those who "devote themselves to myths and endless genealogies. These promote controversies rather than God's work— which is by faith."[21] Such a person "is conceited and understands nothing. He has an unhealthy interest in controversies and quarrels about words that result in envy, strife, malicious talk, evil suspicions and constant friction between men of corrupt mind, who have been robbed of the truth."[22]

These are as much Paul's warnings to those who are following Timothy as they are exhortations to Timothy himself. But in 2 Timothy, the warnings seem to get personal: "Don't have anything to do with foolish and stupid arguments, because you know they produce quarrels. And the Lord's servant must not quarrel; instead, he must be kind to everyone, able to teach, not resentful. Those who oppose him he must gently instruct, in the hope that God will grant them repentance leading them to a knowledge of the truth."[23]

Perhaps Paul realized that Timothy was enjoying "correcting" other people a little too much. There comes a point when we stop teaching and start arguing. It's a fine line, but we need to make sure we don't cross it. Discussions devoid of love—that is, arguments aimed at defeating rather than truly caring for the welfare of the other person—are not godly. "If I have the gift of prophecy and can fathom all mysteries and all knowledge ... but have not love, I am nothing."[24]

Paul was similarly direct with another young leader, Titus. "Avoid foolish controversies and genealogies and arguments and quarrels about the law, because these are unprofitable and useless." Paul saw this divisiveness as a very, very serious sin. "Warn a divisive person once, and then warn him a second time. After that, have nothing to do with him. You may be sure that such a man is warped and sinful; he is self-condemned."[25]

The mark of a Christian is love and grace, not prideful displays of knowledge.

Knowing Rather Than Doing

Intellectuals have to remember that knowing what is right is not a substitute for doing what is right; on the contrary, knowing what is right gives us a greater obligation to bring our life into conformity with our words. James warns that teachers will receive a stricter judgment.[26]

According to the book of Proverbs, the truly wise person is someone who actively applies the ways of righteousness which they have studied to understand. Right thinking is essential to a healthy Christian existence; right action, however, is equally essential.

Being Proud

"Gary," my wife whispered, "you better save the pastor."

We had brought a young man to church who was engaging the pastor in a vigorous discussion, pointing out the "heresy" in the pastor's sermon from just moments before. This young man has a good mind, but it is as critical as it is sharp, and unfortunately his discernment has yet to catch up to his intellect.

> *Knowing what is right is not a substitute for doing what is right.*

Pride is a common failing among those with a superior mind. It is demonstrated by the common desire to correct virtually everyone. Some people seem incapable of refraining from passing judgment on others' intellectual failings. You get the feeling that their sense of self-worth comes from being able to demonstrate their intellectual superiority.

If God has gifted you with an unusually good mind, remember that he has entrusted it to you in order that you might serve the church—not exalt yourself. Someone with a beautiful voice can still be obnoxious if he sings at inappropriate times; and someone with a superior mind can still be offensive if she doesn't learn the time and place to engage others in proper discourse.

Are You an Intellectual?

Are you an intellectual? Score the following statements on a scale of five to one, with five being very true and one being not true at all. Record your answer in the space provided.

_____ 1. I feel closest to God when I learn something new about him that I didn't understand before. My mind needs to be stimulated. It's very important to me that I know exactly what I believe.

_____ 2. I get frustrated when the church focuses too much on feelings and spiritual experience. Of far more importance is the need to understand the Christian faith and have proper doctrine.

_____ 3. The words *concepts* and *truth* are very appealing to me.

_____ 4. I feel close to God when I participate in several hours of uninterrupted study time—reading God's Word or good Christian books and then perhaps having an opportunity to teach (or participate in a discussion with) a small group.

_____ 5. A book on church dogmatics would be appealing to me.

_____ 6. I spend more money on books than music tapes.

The total of all your answers. _____

Any score of fifteen or higher indicates a preference for this spiritual temperament. Record your score in chapter eleven on page 217 so you will have a composite picture of your soul's path to God.

A High Calling

The Christian church has produced some of history's most brilliant thinkers. We don't have to aspire to the heights reached by John Calvin or Blaise Pascal to make an impact, however. Intellectually inclined believers can play a crucial role in the kingdom of God by witnessing to his truth in communities all across the world through adult Sunday school classes, newspaper editorials, and conversations with friends and families.

There was a time in my life when I may have been predominantly an intellectual. I don't believe I'm there now, but I still need the stimulation of a mind that's being captured by God's truth. I'm "fed" by verses that send me into a "deep-thinking" mode, and delighted when someone helps me understand something I didn't understand before.

I guess what it comes down to is that I've never learned something about God that didn't draw me closer to him. I'm confident this could be the testimony of every Christian who earnestly seeks his face by expanding their understanding.

PART THREE

Understanding Your Sacred Pathway

ELEVEN

TENDING THE GARDEN OF THE SOUL

Suppose two women were planting a vegetable garden. On the same day, they prepared the earth and planted their seeds. One then neglected her garden and waited for her vegetables to grow. The other woman worked in her garden regularly. She put cages around the young tomato plants, she drove in sticks beside those vegetable plants that were going to grow up high, and she put netting around plants that were particularly attractive to rabbits and other animals.

Several months later the two women went out for the harvest. One found tomatoes rotting on the ground, beans whose vines had spread among the other plants, weeds that were choking most of the carrots—all of which had been raided by birds and squirrels. She pulled up a handful of food and figured that planting a garden wasn't worth it—the food wasn't as good, the harvest was small, and, well, grocery stores were so much more convenient.

Her neighbor, however, harvested a basketful of good vegetables every other day, which had a better taste than those in the grocery store. She figured that, when everything was added up, she probably saved a good fifteen to twenty percent on her grocery bill during the summer months. Both women planted, but only one tended.

I've known Christians who have committed their lives to following Christ at about the same time; but the influence this commitment had on their lives soon became markedly different. One lived a life of self-absorption. Christianity made sense, but it became almost a convenience—no need to take it too seriously or to reorder one's life around it. The other person, however, took a different approach. She found ways to make Bible study a regular part of her life. She kept her prayer life fresh and varied. New attributes came to the forefront, and before she knew it, people were asking her for advice and counseling. She soon founded a bonafide ministry, almost by accident.

Some of us live with the mistaken impression that our faith needs only to be planted, not tended.

Both planted a spiritual garden, but only one tended.

Some of us live with the mistaken impression that our faith needs only to be planted, not tended. Becoming a mature Christian, some think, is like becoming six feet tall—it either happens or it doesn't. This is not the view of those who have written the classics of our faith or the view of many experienced pastors or teachers. Nor is it the view of Scripture.

A classical spiritual movement in the Middle Ages encouraged Christians to think of their soul as a garden. I hope this book can build on that imagery, helping us tend the garden of our souls by understanding our spiritual temperaments. The first question we need to ask ourselves, then, is "How am I doing?"

It may help you to take a step back and evaluate your current devotional life, beginning with the quiet time. What are you doing now, and how well is it working? Does the prospect of another quiet time excite you? Make you feel guilty? Do your quiet times "build on each other," or are they beginning to feel like more of a burden than a blessing?

Some Christians may find that a traditional quiet time—twenty or thirty minutes of Bible study, followed by twenty or thirty minutes of prayer and worship—is the very best way for them to relate to God ninety percent of the time. These Christians may simply be looking for some supplementary activities for the remaining ten percent of the time. Other Christians may feel they are in need of a complete spiritual overhaul. Understanding their spiritual temperament will greatly affect the content of their devotional time.

Understanding Your Sacred Pathway

Now that you've looked at each of the nine spiritual temperaments, you're ready to determine your spiritual personality. Remember that you will probably have more than one dominant temperament.

Also, spiritual temperaments can evolve over time. Just as a married couple will express their love for each other differently in their fifties than they did in their twenties, so our love relationship with God undergoes changes as we mature and walk through life. The evaluations from chapters two through ten describe where you are right now and what activities you will find most helpful as you seek to grow spiritually today. You can then move on to incorporate and learn from other temperaments.

Just as a married couple will express their love for each other differently in their fifties than they did in their twenties, so our love relationship with God undergoes changes as we mature and walk through life.

You have already filled in your score for each of the temperaments:

_____ Naturalist
_____ Sensate
_____ Traditionalist
_____ Ascetic
_____ Activist
_____ Caregiver
_____ Enthusiast
_____ Contemplative
_____ Intellectual

The higher your score in each category, the more it corresponds to who you are. List each temperament in order of its importance to your life:

Discovering our strong tendencies and predominant spiritual temperament gives us the information we need to construct a comprehensive plan for spiritual growth.

The Interplay of Our Spiritual Temperaments

When I took the above test, I scored strongest in the naturalist category, followed by the intellectual. The ascetic temperament was a strong third. Therefore, I can reasonably assume that, for me to be spiritually healthy, I need to spend a good deal of time out-of-doors (naturalist). Second, I need to engage in activities that challenge my mind (intellectual). Finally, I can be reasonably sure I have a strong need for discipline and solitude (ascetic).

If I were reading this book for the first time, I'd go back and reread the three chapters corresponding to my three strongest temperaments. I could then begin writing a "spiritual prescription," based on some of the suggestions in those chapters. At least once a week, I'll want to spend some time going on a prayer-walk through the woods. On a regular basis, I'll need to make sure I'm continuing to study. Perhaps I'll need to order some more cassette tapes (lectures) to listen to during my afternoon commute. Maybe I'll want to check out the latest Christian book catalog to see if some new titles sound particularly interesting. Also, I should begin respecting my need for discipline and solitude.

I'm not suggesting that we feed our souls only what they want—and risk shrinking them. There is a time and a place for stretching into new experiences, but few of us want to experiment with a new, exotic meal every night. Once we've discovered what draws us into the holy, we can explore new areas of nourishment, knowing there's always something "tried and true" to fall back on.

This gives us a long-term view of Christian spirituality. For example, I sometimes struggle with the demands of a very visible, people-oriented job. I frequently speak at banquets and conferences; and if anything is going to make me feel run down after a while, it's being confined to a cramped hotel room and talking before large groups.

> *I want to faithfully serve God for fifty or sixty or seventy years, which means I need to consider how I can be spiritually replenished.*

Yet my job requires me to do this. It's what God has called me to do now, so I need to make allowances for spiritual nourishment within this context. To keep my sanity, I have to schedule time to get outside when I'm on the road (not a problem at retreats, but more difficult at some conferences), and I almost always reject the idea of sleeping in somebody's house. I need—not just want—time alone, without any demands of propriety or politeness. Otherwise I'll grow frustrated with my responsibilities, and I'll not be able to fulfill my calling.

Some Christians get recharged by getting together and talking about what has happened or just kicking back and enjoying each other's company. I prefer to be alone, to think and pray, and wind down slowly.

I used to struggle with this need, wondering if I was being selfish. However, now I know that if I serve God in a blazing two weeks, or a blazing ten years, and then become burnt out for long periods of time, I will not have been a good steward of my life. I want to faithfully serve God for fifty or sixty or seventy years, which means I need to consider how I can be spiritually replenished.

On his deathbed a great Christian evangelist said, "God gave me a message and a horse to carry that message. I have beaten the horse to death, and now I can no longer carry the message." The horse was his body, but it could also have been his soul.

I've met too many godly men and women who were burnt out before they entered their most productive years. Sometimes burnout led them to quit the ministry and never look back. Others have sought escape through illicit activity and brought scandal on the church of Christ. If God grants it, I want to be serving him just as zealously in my sixties, seventies, and eighties as I am now. Twenty years from now, I don't want to have gained vital and precious experience but have lost my motivation and joy.

If we tend our garden, we'll have plenty of food with which to feed others. If we give our garden just cursory attention, we may have enough to feed just ourselves. If we completely neglect our garden, we're going to be so hungry we'll become "consumer" Christians, feeding off others.

Discovering our spiritual temperament is a means by which we can achieve the desired end—knowing God, and obeying his call on our life. The Puritans called the Sabbath the "market day of the soul," a special day to care for our inner world and to spend extra time relating to our God. The problem is that some of us try to take a shortcut and fulfill God's call without receiving God's nourishment. Disaster lies down those roads. Another temptation is to judge one spiritual temperament as better than another.

Tolerance for Temperaments

During my first year of college I started getting very excited about studying the Bible—not just reading it, but really studying it. I began with the book of Romans, and spent hours poring over the first few verses. Romans 1:1 begins with Paul writing, "Paul, a servant of Jesus Christ, called to be an apostle." This catapulted me into several days' study of the words *servant* and *apostle*. I hadn't studied Greek yet, but I searched through commentaries, concordances, and word studies.

The leader of my small group found out what I was doing and raised some questions. "The best type of Bible study," he said, "is inductive, not deductive. You need to discover for yourself what the Bible means, not have people tell you what it means through commentaries." In his mind, I was breaking a cardinal rule. The "holy" method of Bible study was to sit before an open Bible and interpret it in light of your own experience.

During this time, I was as shortsighted as my leader. I thought a fellow Bible study member was "cheating" because he took walks down by the bay or through the woods and counted them as "quiet times." *That's not a quiet time,* I thought. You had to have an intercessory prayer list and a Bible study notebook to have a real quiet time.

Both my leader and I needed to be more tolerant. Every true spiritual path has Christ at its center, but in Christ there are many ways for us to express our faith. Maybe my Bible study leader didn't like to use commentaries or word studies, but was his method any holier than mine? Was my friend's method of walking by the bay any less holy than my method of praying through a list of family members, fellow Christians, foreign countries, and friends who didn't know the Lord?

I'm hesitant to use the word *tolerance* because it has been so abused today. Tolerance is not the chief virtue that our culture has made it out to be. However, it is an important virtue, especially when you are tolerating different spiritual temperaments.

Different personality types often have a difficult time working and living together. Some mixes are recipes for disaster. But even though we're talking about spiritual temperaments, not personality types, the overall principle is the same. It's difficult for us to understand— and even more difficult to appreciate—people who approach something—in this case, Someone—differently than we do.

We must be careful not to invalidate another's expression of faith simply because it differs from our own. Pastors especially need to be sensitive to the spiritual temperaments of their people. Richard Baxter wrote the all-time classic on pastoral work in the seventeenth century, and *The Reformed Pastor* is still read in many seminaries today as a model of effective pastoral ministry. Baxter stresses the importance of giving individual attention to each church member. The application today, I think, is to respect the ways different people nourish their souls.

As a writer, speaker, and discipler, I've had to try to understand what makes people tick. I must confess, certain spiritual temperaments make me bristle. If I were in a church full of one or two particular temperaments, I think I'd go crazy. But that doesn't mean I believe those spiritual temperaments are any less valid than the ones that predominate in my life.

Parents, your children may love God in a way that is totally different from the way you have learned to love God. Husbands and wives, your spouse may love God in a way you just don't understand. Pastor, your church members may have an altogether different expression of faith than the one with which you are familiar. Can we still respect these "different" Christians? Can we, in Christian humility, encourage others to nurture their souls in ways that are most effective for them as long as they remain true to orthodoxy and the historic Christian faith? I'd hope that we would all answer yes.

A danger related to intolerance is segregation. As I've taught this material in various settings, I've become sensitized to the depth of feeling with which Christians view their favored ways of worshiping God. At one church, a woman came up to me and said, "What am I supposed to do when I realize I'm in the completely wrong church for my temperament?"

We need to learn from each other rather than segregate ourselves within our own confining experiences.

I believe we would seriously impoverish God's church if we created "The First Church of the Activist," "The Second Church of the Traditionalist," or "The Outdoor Chapel of the Naturalist." We need to learn from each other rather than segregate ourselves within our own confining experiences.

I also think people expect entirely too much of their church. A pastor who reviewed this book in its early stages wrote in a margin, "I think you've told me why pastors hear so much criticism of worship services and so little praise; a particular variety of service will only please one-ninth of Christians!"

My pastor friend is right: Each church is full of conflicting temperaments. It is unreasonable to expect everyone's spiritual needs to be fully met by an hour-long service every seven days. It is my hope that this book will make it easier for people to supplement the corporate worship service with their own regular devotions. Then during church they can focus on the corporate call of the Christian faith and how they can reach out to others.

It is idolatry to demand that one teacher give you everything you need to grow in your faith. A pastor is frequently given the charge to teach one hundred or more other individuals, all of whom are in different stages of life, vocation, and faith. It is also questionable to assume that a full life of worship can be developed in just sixty minutes a week of corporate time. If all your worship needs can be met in one hour a week, your need for worship is far too small!

A much more healthy approach is to develop a life of faith, prayer, and worship that feeds into the life of the church. Rather than criticize the church service, learn how to add to it. Maybe your perspective isn't represented, but perhaps those in charge of leading the worship service can learn from your temperament. They may not want to incorporate your suggestion in every worship service, but perhaps they'll consider it every few weeks or so.

I hope this book will teach us that there is more than one spiritual prescription for growth. God is bigger—much, much bigger—than we can possibly know in our own limited experience.

How Does Your Garden Look?

We were made to love God. Think about that for a minute—*we were made to love God.* Like the two gardeners mentioned at the start of this chapter, each of us stands before an open plot of land. God will search heaven and earth to provide us with what we need to plant and maintain a beautiful garden of love, intimacy, and fellowship with him. Not a second of our existence passes without God thinking about how to turn our hearts toward him. Not a single second.

The almost unbelievable joy is that you can enjoy a relationship with God that he will have with no one else. *And God eagerly, passionately, yearns for that relationship to begin.* God is just as eager to love and know you as he was to know Moses, David, and Mary. You are no less precious to him than were these heroes of the faith. But each one of these saints—Moses, David, and Mary—spent time cultivating and growing their relationship with God. Each one made knowing God the chief passion of their heart. Will you respond to that invitation today?

NOTES

Chapter 1: Loving God

1. A. W. Tozer, *The Pursuit of God* (Camp Hill, Penn.: Christian Publications, 1982), 12-13.
2. Morton Kelsey, *Transcend* (Rockport, Mass.: Element, 1981), 122.
3. Annie Dillard, *Holy the Firm* (New York: Harper and Row, 1977).
4. Ibid.
5. W. Phillip Keller, *Taming Tension* (Grand Rapids: Baker, 1979).
6. Francis Schaeffer, *How Shall We Then Live?* (Old Tappan: Revell, 1976).
7. "Mother Teresa of Calcutta," *Charlotte Observer* (June 14, 1995).
8. Ibid.
9. J. I. Packer, *Knowing God* (Downers Grove: InterVarsity, 1973).
10. J. I. Packer, *Keep in Step with the Spirit* (Old Tappan: Revell, 1984).
11. Susan Power Bratton, *Christianity, Wilderness and Wildlife* (Scranton: University of Scranton Press, 1993), 78.

Chapter 2: Naturalists

1. Waynes Simsic, *Natural Prayer* (Mystic, Conn.: Twenty-Third, 1991), 70.
2. Bratton, *Christianity, Wilderness and Wildlife*, 35.
3. Matthew 4:13.
4. Matthew 4:18.
5. Bratton, *Christianity, Wilderness and Wildlife*, 244. I want to credit Susan Power Bratton for her quote, "Baptism is moved from the river to the marble font, the calling of disciples is shifted from the seaside to formal ordination services, and prayer is moved from the isolated place to the packed church pew," which I have adapted for this book.
6. Conrad Cherry, *Nature and Religious Imagination* (Philadelphia: Fortress, 1980), 26.
7. Roger D. Sorrell, *St. Francis of Assisi and Nature* (New York: Oxford University Press, 1988), 29.
8. Bratton, *Christianity, Wilderness and Wildlife*, 165
9. Quotes taken from Paul Hoversten, "Flight Through Heavens Awes Glenn," *USA Today* (November 2, 1998), and Seth Broenstein, "Astronauts Find God in Space," *Tacoma News Tribune* (November 7, 1998).
10. Psalm 19:1.
11. Romans 1:20.
12. John Milton, *Paradise Lost*, V, 511.

13. Bratton, *Christianity, Wilderness and Wildlife*, 90–91.

14. Ibid., 93.

15. Mark 6:30–32.

16. Margaret Ruth Miles, cited in H. Paul Santmire, *The Travail of Nature* (Philadelphia: Fortress, 1985).

17. Sermons on the Gospel of John, cited in Santmire, *The Travail of Nature*, 131.

18. Ibid., 130.

19. Bonaventure, cited in Santmire, *The Travail of Nature*, 99.

20. I want to credit Susan Power Bratton for many of the insights contained in this section.

21. My thanks to the Reverend Brian Thorstad for his comments here.

Chapter 3: Sensates

1. Henri Nouwen, *The Return of the Prodigal Son* (New York: Doubleday, 1994), 3–5.

2. Ibid.

3. Ezekiel 1:4, 26–27.

4. Ezekiel 3:12-13.

5. Ezekiel 3:1–3, 15.

6. Ezekiel 43:2.

7. Revelation 1:10, 14–17.

8. Von Ogden Vogt, *Art and Religion,* (New Haven: Yale University Press, 1921), 145ff.

9. Ibid., 148, 152.

10. Ibid., 56.

11. Harold Best, *Music Through the Eyes of Faith* (New York: HarperCollins, 1993), 185.

12. Philip Whitfield and Mike Stoddart, *Hearing, Taste and Smell: Pathways of Perception* (New York: Torstar, 1985), 63.

13. Exodus 25:6.

14. Exodus 30:7.

15. Malachi 1:11.

16. Matthew 2:11.

17. Luke 1:9–11.

18. 2 Kings 22:17; Jeremiah 1:16.

19. Isaiah 1:13.

20. Whitfield and Stoddart, *Hearing, Taste and Smell*, 153.

21. Ibid., 156.

22. Nouwen, *The Return of the Prodigal Son*, 4.

23. Michael Long, "The Sense of Sight," *National Geographic* (November 1992), 8.

24. Exodus 35:31.

25. Vogt, *Art and Religion*, 206.

26. Ibid., 205–6.

27. Henry Morgan, ed., *Approaches to Prayer* (Harrisburg, Penn.: More-house, 1991), 92.

28. Whitfield and Stoddart, *Hearing, Taste and Smell*, 85.

29. Vogt, *Art and Religion*, 77–78.

Chapter 4: Traditionalists

1. "CT Talks to Kathleen Norris," *Christianity Today* (November 22, 1993), 36.

2. Genesis 12:7–8; 13:18.

3. Exodus 20:23–24; 40:12.

4. Leviticus 10:8–11.

5. Leviticus 10:1–2; 16:1.

6. Exodus 25:40; Hebrews 8:5.

7. Ezra 7:16; 8:21, 35; 10:7, 11; Nehemiah 8:3.

8. Luke 4:16; Acts 3:1; 16:13; 21:26.

9. Evelyn Underhill, *Worship* (New York: Harper and Row, 1936), 20.

10. Gertrud Mueller Nelson, *To Dance with God: Family Ritual and Community Celebration* (New York: Paulist, 1986), 25.

11. Ibid., 2–26.

12. Walter Wangerin, *Reliving the Passion* (Grand Rapids: Zondervan, 1992).

13. Joshua 1:8.

14. Joseph Jungmann, *Christian Prayer Through the Centuries*, trans. by John Coyne (New York: Paulist, 1978), 30.

15. Underhill, *Worship*, 69–72.

16. Jungmann, *Christian Prayer Through the Centuries*, 8.

17. Ibid., 9.

18. Eberhard Bethge, ed., *Letters and Papers from Prison* (New York: Macmillan, 1972), 203.

19. Numbers 15:37–40.

20. Sidney Heath, *The Romance of Symbolism* (London: Francis Griffiths, 1909), 57–61.

21. Ibid., 116.

22. Ibid., 117–20.

23. Ibid., 157–58.

24. Ibid., 194–99.

25. Ibid., 214–15.

26. Numbers 21:4-8; 2 Kings 18:4.

27. Nelson, *To Dance with God*, 7.

28. W. A. Van Gemeren, "Offerings and Sacrifices in Bible Times," *Evangelical Dictionary of Theology*, Walter Elwell, ed. (Grand Rapids: Baker, 1984), 788.

29. Underhill, *Worship*, 53.

30. Romans 3:25; 8:3; 12:1.

31. Amos 5:21–24.

32. Jeremiah 7:4–7.

33. Matthew 23:27.

34. Acts 10.

35. Colossians 2:16–17.

36. 1 Timothy 4:1–5.

37. Underhill, *Worship*, 31.

Chapter 5: Ascetics

1. Numbers 6.

2. Matthew 4:1; 6:5–6, 16–17; 14:13, 22–23.

3. Mark 1:35.

4. Matthew 26:36.

5. Daniel 9:3.

6. Joel 1:13–14; 2:12.

7. M. Basil Pennington, *A Place Apart: Monastic Prayer and Practice for Everyone* (New York: Doubleday, 1983), 26.

8. Ibid., 26.

9. Sorrell, *St. Francis of Assisi and Nature*, 20.

10. Underhill, *Worship*, 164.

11. Philip Rousseau, *Ascetics, Authority, and the Church: In the Age of Jerome and Cassian* (London: Oxford University Press, 1978), 48.

12. Ibid., 117.

13. Ibid., 100.

14. Bratton, *Christianity, Wilderness and Wildlife*, 181.

15. Felix Duffey, *Psychiatry and Asceticism* (London: B. Herder, 1950), 60.

16. Ibid., 60–61.

17. Ibid., 62.

18. Rousseau, *Ascetics, Authority, and the Church*, 26–27.

19. Augustine, *City of God*, XIX.vi.

20. Rousseau, *Ascetics, Authority, and the Church*, 153.

21. Pennington, *A Place Apart*, 41.

22. Ibid., 43.

23. Ibid., 65.

24. Ibid., 111.

25. Zechariah 7:1–10.

26. Mark 6:30–32.

27. Isaiah 64:6

Chapter 6: Activists

1. Exodus 2:11–12.
2. Exodus 2:17.
3. Exodus 3:11–12.
4. Exodus 18:14.
5. Exodus 17:4.
6. 1 Kings 18:22; 19:10.
7. 1 Kings 19:4; 18:22.
8. 2 Kings 8:11–13.
9. Habakkuk 1:2, 4.
10. Habakkuk 2:4.
11. Ibid.
12. John 4:34.
13. Francis Schaeffer, *The Mark of the Christian: The Complete Works of Francis Schaeffer* (Westchester: Crossway, 1982).
14. Ibid.
15. Thomas Merton, *What Is Contemplation?* (London: Burns, Oates, and Washbourne, 1950), 14–15.
16. Francis Schaeffer, *Bad News for Modern Man* (Westchester, Ill.: Crossway, 1984), 94.
17. Klaus Bockmuehl, *Books: God's Tools in the History of Salvation* (Moscow, Ind.: Community Christian Ministries, 1992).
18. Charles Colson, *Loving God* (Grand Rapids: Zondervan, 1996), 96.
19. Schaeffer, *Bad News for Modern Man*, 96.
20. Ibid., 106–7.
21. Jungmann, *Christian Prayer Through the Centuries*, 148.
22. 1 Samuel 30:22.
23. 1 Samuel 30:23.
24. Paul Carter, *The Decline and Revival of the Social Gospel* (Ithica, N.Y.: Cornel University Press, 1954), 82.
25. Matthew 7:1–5.

Chapter 7: Caregivers

1. Esther 2:11.
2. Esther 4:1.
3. Esther 4:13–14.
4. Esther 8:7–8.
5. Esther 9:20, 22.
6. Esther 10:3.
7. Matthew 4:23–24; 6:2; 9:35–36.
8. Matthew 14:14.

9. 1 John 3:14.

10. 1 John 3:17.

11. Philippians 2:4.

12. Hebrews 6:10.

13. Hebrews 13:2.

14. James 1:27.

15. 1 Peter 4:9–10.

16. Ezekiel 16:49.

17. Steve Sjogren, *Conspiracy of Kindness* (Ann Arbor: Servant, 1993).

18. Robert Wuthnow, *Acts of Compassion* (Princeton: Princeton University Press, 1991), 87.

19. Ibid., 105.

20. Ibid., 128–29.

21. Luke 10:38–42.

22. Wuthnow, *Acts of Compassion,* 104.

23. Ibid., 106.

24. 1 Timothy 5:8.

Chapter 8: Enthusiasts

1. Deuteronomy 18:14–16.

2. Acts 3:19–26.

3. 1 Samuel 13:12.

4. Genesis 28:10–15; 37:1–11; 1 Kings 3:5–10; Daniel 7:1.

5. Joel 2:28.

6. Matthew 1:20; 2:12.

7. Acts 9:3–9, 10–16; 10:3–6, 9–18; 16:9.

8. Kelsey, *Transcend,* 54–57.

9. John Wesley, May 20, 1739.

10. John Wesley, November 25, 1759.

11. Genesis 41:15; Daniel 2:17–19.

12. Genesis 37:5; Acts 16:9–10.

13. Kelsey, *Transcend,* 55.

14. Deuteronomy 16:13–15.

15. 2 Samuel 6:22.

16. 1 Chronicles 15:16.

17. 1 Chronicles 13:8.

18. 2 Chronicles 29:26.

19. Matthew 26:30.

20. Luke 19:37–40.

21. Acts 16:25; Ephesians 5:19.

22. Revelation 7:10; Revelation 19:1, 6.

23. Acts 3:1.

24. 1 Corinthians 14:40.

25. Acts 8:9–24.

26. 1 Chronicles 13:9–10.

27. 1 Chronicles 16:9, 30.

28. Nehemiah 8:10.

29. Matthew 18:3; 19:14.

30. Underhill, *Worship*.

31. Ibid., 179.

32. Kelsey, *Transcend*, 34.

Chapter 9: Contemplatives

1. Deuteronomy 33:12.

2. Deuteronomy 7:7–8.

3. Psalm 63:1, 3, 5, 6, 8.

4. Song of Songs 2:4–5.

5. Song of Songs 3:1–4.

6. Isaiah 29:13.

7. Jeremiah 2:2.

8. Matthew 26:6–13.

9. Luke 10:38–42.

10. Gary Thomas, *Seeking the Face of God* (Eugene, Ore.: Harvest House, 1999).

11. Thomas Merton, *Contemplation in a World of Action*, (Garden City, N.Y.: Image Books, 1973), 6, 9.

12. Ibid., 9–10.

13. Dom Cuthbert Butler, *Western Mysticism: The Teaching of Augustine, Gregory and Bernard on Contemplation and the Contemplative Life* (London: Constable, 1922), 26.

14. John 15:15.

15. Merton, *What Is Contemplation?*, 5.

16. Jungmann, *Christian Prayer through the Centuries*, 44.

17. Dr. Gabriele Winkler, *Prayer Attitude in the Eastern Church* (Minneapolis: Life and Life, 1978), 13.

18. Ibid., 18–19.

19. Matthew 12:43–45.

20. See Thomas, *Seeking the Face of God*, 181ff.

21. M. Basil Pennington, *Daily We Touch Him* (Garden City, N.Y.: Doubleday, 1977), 51–52.

Chapter 10: Intellectuals

1. Kelsey, *Transcend*, 37.

2. Jungmann, *Christian Prayer Through the Centuries*, 114.

3. Deuteronomy 33:10.

4. 1 Kings 3:3.

5. 1 Kings 4:33–34.

6. Psalm 49:1–4.

7. Proverbs 1:5–7.

8. Proverbs 2:3–4.

9. Proverbs 4:7.

10. Luke 2:46–47, 52.

11. Matthew 22:37.

12. I am indebted to Dr. Donald Lewis of Regent College, Vancouver, B.C., for bringing many of these titles to my attention.

13. Kenneth Scott Latourette, *History of Christianity* (San Francisco: Harper, 1975).

14. Robert Clouse, Richard V. Pierard, and Edwin M. Yamauchi, *Two Kingdoms: The Church and Culture Through the Ages* (Chicago: Moody Press, 1993).

15. Daniel Reid, *Dictionary of Christianity in America* (Downers Grove: InterVarsity, 1990).

16. Mark Noll, *A History of Christianity in the United States and Canada* (Grand Rapids: Eerdmans, 1992).

17. David Wells, *Eerdmans' Handbook to Christianity in America* (Grand Rapids: Eerdmans).

18. Dorothy Sayers, *Creed or Chaos?* (New York: Harcourt Brace, 1949).

19. Ibid., 28.

20. Acts 23:1–5.

21. 1 Timothy 1:4.

22. 1 Timothy 6:4–5.

23. 2 Timothy 2:23–25.

24. 1 Corinthians 13:23.

25. Titus 3:9–11.

26. James 3:1.

For information about the Center for Evangelical Spirituality,
write:

Center for Evangelical Spirituality
P.O. Box 29417
Bellingham, WA 98228–1427
GLT3@aol.com
www.garythomas.com

Sacred Marriage

*What If God Designed Marriage to Make Us
Holy More Than to Make Us Happy?*

Gary Thomas

"This isn't a book that seeks to tell you how to
have a happier marriage. This is a book that looks
at how we can use the challenges, joys, struggles,
and celebrations of marriage to draw closer to
God." —Gary Thomas

Scores of books have been written that offer
guidance for building the marriage of your
dreams. But what if God's primary intent for
your marriage isn't to make you happy . . . but
holy? And what if your relationship isn't as much
about you and your spouse as it is about you and God? *Sacred
Marriage* invites you to view your marriage in a new and different light,
as a spiritual discipline, a means whereby you can come to know God more
fully and intimately.

Gary Thomas writes, "The ultimate purpose of this book is not to make
you love your spouse more—though I think that will happen along the way.
It's to equip you to love your God more and to help you reflect the character of his Son more precisely."

Historically, the "deeper walk" has been considered the province of the
celibate, of saints and ascetics, monks and nuns. But the Bible, in depict-
ing God's passionate, holy relationship with his people, is filled with images
of the bridegroom and the bride and of a husband with his wife. Everything
about your marriage—everything—is filled with prophetic potential, with
the capacity for discovering and revealing Christ's character.

The respect you accord your partner; the forgiveness you humbly seek
and graciously extend; the ecstasy, awe, and sheer fun of lovemaking; the
history you and your mate build with one another—in these and other
facets of your marriage, *Sacred Marriage* uncovers the mystery of God's over-
arching purpose. Like no other spiritual discipline, marriage reveals your
deep need to draw strength and life from Jesus Christ alone; consequently,
it is unsurpassed for releasing his character and vision in your life.

Sacred Marriage may very well alter profoundly the contours of your marriage. It will almost certainly change you. Because whether it is delightful
or difficult, your marriage can become a doorway to a closer walk with God
and to a spiritual integrity that, like salt, seasons the world around you with
the savor of Christ.

Pick up your copy today at your local Christian bookstore!

Hardcover 0-310-22796-8
Softcover 0-310-24282-7

Authentic Faith

The Power of a Fire-Tested Life

Gary L. Thomas

What if life wasn't meant to be perfect but we were meant to trust the One who is?

Isn't it startling how God reveals himself most profoundly in places we least expect to encounter him? He is intent on showing himself Lord in all our circumstances—in the highs and the lows alike.

Best-selling author Gary Thomas helps us sharpen our spiritual vision and fortify our commitment by examining eleven disciplines God uses to forge a fire-tested faith. A biblical view of these disciplines can safeguard us from disillusionment when—not if—difficulties surface in our lives. How we respond will determine the depth and vitality of our walk with God.

Sharing scriptural insights, the wisdom of Christians through the centuries, and cogent personal observations, Thomas explores the disciplines of:

- Selflessness
- Waiting
- Suffering
- Persecution
- Social Mercy
- Forgiveness
- Mourning
- Contentment
- Sacrifice
- Hope and Fear

As Gary Thomas reminds us, Jesus said that in this world we will have trouble. Paul exhorted believers to mourn with those who mourn. James wrote that God chooses the poor of this world to be rich in faith. Clearly, faith is about something other than a smooth ride through this fallen world. Rather, authentic faith is shaped, tempered, and purified in the flames of struggle.

Authentic Faith reveals the rich benefits that derive from embracing the harder truths of Scripture. This eye-opening look at what it means to be a true disciple of Jesus will encourage you, bolster your faith, and help you rise above shallow attachments to fix your heart on things of eternal worth.

Hardcover 0-310-23692-4

Pick up a copy at your favorite bookstore today!

ZONDERVAN

GRAND RAPIDS, MICHIGAN 49530

www.zondervan.com

We want to hear from you. Please send your comments about this book to us in care of the address below. Thank you.

ZONDERVAN™

GRAND RAPIDS, MICHIGAN 49530

WWW.ZONDERVAN.COM